Dream catcher

ARTS COUNCIL ENGLAND

fcbs.biz
... putting the wiz into your biz!

Introduction

Welcome, readers, to issue 14 of *Dream Catcher*. It seems like yesterday that this business of producing a literary journal started. But it was nine years ago, before 11.09.01, before the millennium, before so much. Then it was dream. I thought: maybe we'll produce a few issues for the college of Ripon and York St John, now called York St John College, and then retire into happy obscurity like many small poetry magazines. Now we have for the second year running a poet short listed for the Forward Prize for Poetry in the single poem category. In this year's Forward Book of Poetry we have two representatives: Mandy Coe's 'The Weight of Cows' (from issue 12) in the highly recommended section and Mario Susko's 'Conversation' (from issue 13) short listed for the Prize. Nine years ago recognition was a fantasy, now it's a reality and no less strange for that. Congratulation to both writers. Mandy Coe's collection called *The Weight of Cows* is reviewed in this issue and we have another poem from Mario Susko, 'A Refugee Concept'.

Looking back to beginnings, I remember, and wish to thank, those who helped make the dream come true. Anne Price, head of the English School, and David Pierce, senior lecturer, who guided the publication through its early years. Steve Dearden of Yorkshire Arts who recommended funding support, recognising our commitment and promise; Ian Parks who came from no where to encourage better and better writers to submit their work to *Dream Catcher*, broadening the pool of writers we could call on for live literature events. Joe Warner who, from the background, has kept doing necessary tasks from organising printing of leaflets to handling the influx of post. Barbara Harrison who has kept an eye on finances, producing annual accounts or on demand and helping with the proof-reading. Chris Firth who as fiction editor has attracted a higher quality of short story than previously appeared in *Dream Catcher.* I wish to thank our sponsors Freedom Computer Business Services whose support has been far more than financial, Endpapers who help us with distribution, especially to Borders Bookshops around the UK, and all the companies and individuals who have placed ads - some still doing so - augmenting income and keeping us in the black. I want to thank Adrian Tellwright for his unfailing efforts in carrying on the Dream Catcher Creative Writing Workshop in York. Also a special thanks to Ian McMillan, our patron, who inconspicuously and constantly promotes *Dream Catcher.* Sue Stewart, past Literature Officer of the East Midlands, who when *Dream Catcher* moved to Lincoln championed the publication. Maxiprint, who since issue 6 has helped us produce a quality product. Without the support of these significant others my individual determination to bring *Dream Catcher* to national notice would have counted little.

Things change. Chris Firth, after his incredible work for issue 13, has made a side-way move from fiction editor to a consultant editor and Barbara Harrison has decided that someone else needs to corral the finances. Peter Lewin, Ian Parks and Jenny Clarkson have become the main poetry editors while I concentrate on selecting fiction which now is represented to almost the same extent as poetry.

Unlike issues 12 and 13, issue 14 has no theme but to emphasises UK writers. Yet, our international contacts have produced new contributors and I would like to welcome the Algerian writer Amari Hamadene and Ece Sakar from Turkey to the pages of *Dream Catcher.*

Since I moved to Lincoln in 2000, *Dream Catcher* has found a home in the East Midlands literary scene. Since 2003 we have been part of the East Midlands Small Press Consortium. With Five Leaves and Shoestring presses and *Staple* and *Poetry Nottingham International* magazines, we promote small press publications through the region. All this suggests *Dream Catcher* might be around for a few years yet, but only if you - the readers - keep reading.

Paul Sutherland
Founding Editor
September 2004

Contents - Authors

Contents - Authors

Contents - Authors

Dream catcher

Cover Illustration: Ian Emberson

Featured Artist: Ian Emberson

ISSN 1466-9455

Featured Artist
Ian Emberson

Ian Emberson works both as a writer and as an artist. In the former capacity he has had seven books published including his novel in verse *Pirouette of Earth*. Several composers have set his poetry, and Daniel Bath's opera *The Forest* is based on one of his short plays. As an artist he is best known for his postcards and book illustrations.

The drawings in this issue of *Dream Catcher* have been produced by a process Ian Emberson has worked out for himself which he calls 'pseudo scraperboard'.

The Drawings are:

page 24 **It will be a Good Harvest** (comes from the artist's prose-poem *The Comet of 1811*)

page 61 **The Fifth Day of Creation** (a title of one of the artist's poems)

page 80 **The Snake and the Star** (title of one of the aritist's prose-poems)

page 103 **Your World of Solemn Light** (a quote from Emily Bront's poem *Stars*)

page 113 **Beyond the Branches of that Oak** (a quote from the artist's short play *The Forest*)

The Mermaid Chair

Carved in a bench of this church in Zennor,
she seems to ripen from the wood.

Her breasts are bare, but she is wise
& therefore folds

an emerald veil about her hips,
knowing the sight of what she hides

must prove too much for any man.
Of many forms, she rises

from her dark sea bed
to surface through the centuries:

called Magdalene once
though more often found

numbered among the nameless ones.
Monks in the Middle Ages sought

to net her in theology, her
doubleness made to symbolise

Christ's dual nature, God & man.
But she was having none of it,

back in the world
before you could spit,

the fish stink of her everywhere,
nothing that doesn't taste of her:

always already
somewhere else, she's

slipperier than any eel,
astonishing our empty hands.

And she excites
what always was beyond

words
      before this,

her salty trace, alluvial,
delighting our tongues like a new language.

The Mermaid Chair is to be found in the side chapel of St Senara's church, Zennor

Tony Flynn

VILLANELLE

You thought you'd know her by your dying day.
How green her eyes, so dark her voice and low.
You won't admit the memories that stay.

Do those years count? You'd thought there was a way.
You had such friends and plans. Your watch was slow.
You thought you'd know her till your dying day.

The windows you looked out of — kids at play.
The blossom on the cherry. Was it snow?
You cannot hug the memories that stay.

You kept no record of what was to pay.
The zeroes mounted, no line drawn below.
And to your credit just a dying day.

No glass can mirror absence turning grey.
And what you see is nothing much to show.
You do not choose the memories that stay.

Whatever you betrayed time will betray.
The fonts outlast the names of friend or foe.
You do not want the memories to stay.
You thought you'd love her till your dying day.

Peter Dale

I DO

I lay under you,
the passion of the moment
watching telly next door.

The aroma of our love
is the sweat of your
hard day at work.

You mutter empty
sweet nothings
you do not mean.

I've memorised the ceiling.
The cracks you ignore
that I have to notice

look back down at me,
the way you always
avoid doing.

You get off and
collapse onto sheets
that need cleaning.

I shift awkwardly
to the bathroom,
muscles clenched, and wash

the waste of time
from between my tired thighs
and wonder quietly

where it all went wrong.

Jessica Philips

RIGHT

You are right and I am wrong,
completely and unquestionably wrong.

It is true that I thought I was right
and that, therefore, you were wrong

but I was mistaken. I hold up my hands.
You know best. I say this without irony.

You are right and I am wrong.
I take this on board. Fair cop, guv,

and all that. So what do you say
to a clean slate tomorrow,

no hard feelings, beginning anew?
No shadow of what is past, no ill residue

of that time when I thought - could have sworn -
that I was right and you were wrong?

For that was how it seemed. I make no apology.
We can be adult about this. I was right

and you were most definitely wrong
or that was how it seemed.

You were pig-headed (or so it seemed)
and quarrelsome and never entertained

my point of view. God knows, I tried.
I was reasonable and temperate

but your course was set and that was that.
Now that I've agreed (without prejudice)

that you are right and I am blindingly wrong,
perhaps that you'll be good enough to concede this:

no offence intended, but you've been stupid,
insensitive and bloody-minded. If truth were told,

if you could look back with the benefit of hindsight
and mature objectivity. I have the feeling

you'd admit to this. But, hey, water under the bridge,
what's done is done, time the healer,

and all that. What does it matter
if the truth is, you were wrong and I was right?

We can be adult about this. I bear no grudge.
But if I were you, and this is not putting it too strongly,

I'd wonder how I could live with myself,
having perpetrated the hideous lie

that, sure as day follows night,
I was wrong and you were right.

Alan Dunnett

UNTITLED

Kisses blown across oceans
Are helpless as
Butterflies thrown from ships

Paul Nicholson

The Day After

Who says our lovers are
The twins of our mothers…
That it's a matter of course
The style we got used to?
Her kisses on our forehead…
Her arms…
We try to reproduce hundreds of times
Her infinite trials to get rid of us!

The girl inside now
Is sittin' on top of a rock
At the top of a mountain on a lost island
Long hair flowin'
And her tears dried by
The wind…

There's no peace in solitude
Though war is over…
The girl inside now
Is broken.
Hope in a lost heart is unacceptable…
No more dreams of lovers;
Getting used to living
with her own absence…

It is said we got used to being rejected
While loved by our primary love.
Is it because I've felt more and more
Dependent — that your ignorance lasts?
Is it because I've needed you so much…
Can it be true:
Self destructing myself to punish you?

Ece Sakar
translated from Turkish by the author

Autumn Beach

The air is cool
yet the sun feels hot on my cheek.
The glare is blinding
so I close my eyes for a moment.
I inhale deeply
and the strong smell of seaweed
assaults me, making me gasp.
I dig my foot into cold
soggy sand; wrap my toes
around a smooth, flat pebble.

He puts his arms around me
and I snuggle into the soft
woolly warmth of his jumper.
I taste the salt on his lips
as I listen to the rhythmic gush
of the waves,
and watch
a yellow buoy bobbing
some distance from the shore.

Louise Mansfield

Slyvan Exotic

He went back to drafting policies for his country
but never forgot the courtesan in the Arabic play.
She wrote him missives on sheets folded
in triangles like betel leaves
but did not wait for the beloved and spring;
creepers soothed her, her lamp-lit hours passed
among the scented shadows of lovers.

Amari Hamadene
translated from Arabic by David Van de Kamp and the author

To Die For

Fragment 31

Your presence, paradisic, your close
Proximity, the eastern lilt of your delighful
Voice contains a smile and laughter that
Make my heart leap;

And even as I catch your eye my mouth
Runs dry and words escape me as I flush
Deep red, a haze appears instead of sight;
To my confused distress

Your words no longer making any sense, my
Shaking limbs, my breasts weep with pouring
Perspiration, the blood drains from my face;
For you I'd die.

Sappho
adapted by Helen Goodway
from a translation by Robert Chandler

Head of a Kore in a Marble Mine on Paros

As though I had dreamed and woke
In the locus of dreaming, that in my lap,
And like a blind man feeling

Assured myself of her smile. Now I must fag
That weight and my own
Up the steep diagonal. I could remember

Swifts over pools of lupins and see
On the small square of blue daylight
The clean silver dip and lift of one bare fig branch.

More galleries went down behind my back
Like bad thoughts to their hell
And I must fag up the infinite diagonal,

The girl's head heavier and heavier on my heart.

David Constantine

DAVID CONSTANTINE INTERVIEWED BY IAN PARKS

IP: I'm interested in the connection you make between poetry and memory. Could you reiterate what you said during your lecture (Liverpool University, 16 October, 2003) regarding this theme — and say something about how it affects your practice as a poet?

DC: The Mother of the Muses, which is to say the source of all forms of the poetic imagination, was Mnemosyne, Goddess of Memory. In both the writing and reading of poetry, memory and imagination are engaged. As we read, we quicken the effect of the poem; we enable it to excite and enlarge our imaginative sympathy, and we do this by engaging the resources of our lives up to that point. That is why reading a poem often feels like remembering. We realise something; recognise it. Older poetics — with the concept (almost a doctrine) of *inventio* — taught that the writing of a poem was an uncovering of something already there; it was not the invention, out of nothing, of things that had never been. In that sense, the poet was directed to the commonplaces, to the places where things of value were stored in memory. That idea — the intrinsic connection of memory and imagination — is behind much of my practice. And deriving from it, a particular application of it: my writing is often an act of memorialising; of giving things, places and people their due. Especially when I feel that due had not been sufficiently given and may not be. I feel responsible, that I must try to dignify, show the dignity of, lives not sufficiently recognised. But also to memorialise the bad, to make it known, not to allow it to be forgotten. Loss of memory entails a loss of identity. A poem, made of memory and imagination has a very definite identity and so may combat the loss of it in human lives.

IP: You mentioned in the lecture your 'love of places'. The connection between memory and place is certainly a profound one in your work. Could you expand on that here by saying which places specifically? And why?

DC: Several localities in Britain are of vital importance to me; the North-West where I was born and grew up; North-Wales where we always took our holidays; Cornwall and the Scillies where my wife's people come from. Outside Britain, certain areas of France, Italy and Greece. I feel myself to be composed of the places I have inhabited; they are like a very substantial personal literature — everything I have read that mattered. In poems, they are perhaps their chief source of imagery. I want a poetry rooted in this earth and very often the images for it have seemed to me, physically present in the localities I know and love best. I connect memory and imagination with a third resource or impulse: gratitude. I feel grateful to the places that have shaped and nourished my life.

IP: I understand that you'll be taking over the editorship (with Helen Constantine) of *Modern Poetry and Translation*. Could you indicate why translation is so important to you?

DC: Translation matters for poets in two ways. First, very obviously, it gives them access to poetry in languages they do not speak. This is especially beneficial to English-speaking poets. The hegemony of English and American-English brings grave disadvantages with it. Secondly, poets themselves, if they have any ability in any foreign language, should do some translating of its poetry. I don't mean with an eye to publication, I mean for the good it will do them in their mother tongue. It always used to be urged on young poets that they should spend time translating. It was viewed as a sort of journeyman period abroad, after which they would better understand the language of home. You learn what your language can and can't do; what it can perhaps be induced or forced to do, when you are trying to render the movement, argument, feeling, rhythm of a foreign poem. Translation will also help you through the periods, in my case quite long periods, when you cannot write verse at all in your own voice. It is an exercise, keeps you in trim, keeps you in touch at least with a letter until the spirit comes again.

IP: You were at Oxford when Robert Graves was Professor of Poetry there. What is it, in particular, about Graves the poet that makes him such an attractive figure for you?

DC: I went to Grave's lectures, heard him elsewhere whenever I could, and read his poems and his essays. I thought him the real thing, what a poet should be like. I read him again, all his poems and *The White Goddess*, a couple of years ago for a lecture I gave at the Poetry School, and recognised and acknowledged my continuing love and debt. One thing I have from him is the belief that the language of poetry should be at least as rigorous as the language of writing in prose. The other, in my version, is belief in the Muse. I see his faults — he became very formulaic — but several of his poems have mattered vitally to me for more than forty years. I sympathise with him in his loves and terrors.

IP: To go back, if I may, to something you said earlier about giving people and places 'their due'. It reminds me of what Geoffrey Hill once said in relation to his meditations on history. Which individuals do you feel have needed to be given their due?

DC: This came from thinking about my grandmother who was widowed in the First World War. I wanted to tell quite insistently, what ordinary working people suffered. Though I knew nothing firsthand about war, I knew a lot about my grandmother, and felt not only entitled to write about her but also that it was my responsibility. In addition, one way or another, I have had a lot to do with homeless people and with people in psychiatric hospitals. Mostly they seemed not to be speaking for themselves and sometimes I thought I might for them. But by giving people their due I don't just mean indicating how they suffer or how marginalized they might be. I think that on the whole most people do not have a good enough idea of themselves; they are too at the mercy of the belittling images offered by managers, politicians and the media. I think poetry can quicken a better life in people. It can alert them to more various, passionate and engaged ways of being in the world. In that sense it might help them to their due.

IP: I'd like, finally, to concentrate for a moment on a specific poem — 'Watching for Dolphins' from the collection of the same title — which seems to me to encapsulate everything that makes your work distinctive: its sureness of voice and tone together with a complete identification with the subject in hand. It has an almost mystic quality about it. How far do you feel interest in the classical world has influenced your work?

DC: I lived in Greece, on Aigina, with my family for some months. I was writing a book about the early travellers to Greece. We always looked out for dolphins when we were out on the boats. Sometimes we were lucky sometimes we were not. The poem is about hope and longing, disappointed on that occasion. Also about the innocence human beings are capable of. I love the expression on their faces when they are watching and hoping for that sight from the sea. They want an epiphany, in modern times, out of ‘the abused Aegean’. That seems to me a noble desire and not hopeless. I owe Greece a great deal, its land and sea but also, equally, its classical past, in which I have steeped myself, for my academic work and for my poetry. The myths are vital, they seem to me true figures, structures and relations, they recur. I like tradition, continuity and endless metamorphosis in poetry. Greek myths and the genres, forms and texts of Greek literature are like a wellhead, still abundant. They are not the only such sources, but they have been especially important to me. Thanks for your time and patience.

IP: Thanks for yours. It’s been a pleasure.

Cover me, she says

Cover me, she said.

Her voice awakened
a cold passion
and inexplicable love.

Cover me, she said.

I smiled at her.
The asteroids in collision,
light-years from here, entered
the mystery-space of my mind;
I read the explosion
in the surrender of her body.

Cover me, she pleaded,
soft, ardently.

To her third supplication
I pulled the white sheet
over her again
and quietly wept

the loss of a thousand asteroids.

Amari Hamadene
translated from the French by the author

BONDS

Between the flowers and the passing hours
There should be a space to talk about
Sleeping in handcuffs, waking up

With your back on fire, in agony, not through
Arthritis, or a sporting injury, but courtesy
Of tarmac in the carpark the night before.

There should be a place to talk about
Carpet burns on your knees, and the time
You couldn't sit down for a week.

When the vampire bit your neck it was just
A question of passion, and how best
To mark you as possessed, how best

To mark your memory, to draw out
The time of you inside me. To turn brief
Thoughtless encounters into something

You'll never forget. Here's the first time
My lover shaved me, here's the original dirty
Picture, legs spread wide — in this messy

Temporary bedroom, loud the soft click
Of the closing of the door, where the
Only word that's needed is goodbye.

Anne Brechin

Embryo

My brother and sister and I play
in the sandbox. She builds a castle,
roads, a village, directs the baby

in the motherly tone of a firstborn,
keeps him busy, satisfies him
with the belief that he is helping.

I sit opposite, bring handfuls
of the dark underlayer to light,
let it fall in clumps to the ground.

Claire Sharpe

I'LL BE WAITING FOR YOU ON THE OTHER SIDE

She only meant she'd turned 40.
I'll send a belated birthday present.
She was kind not to mention I hadn't tonight
during another of our infrequent flat phonecalls.

Every six months, we talk of the same stuff,
how she'll come back, she'll face her debts.
But it's strange how much absence can effect love,
how much that line reminds me of death.

In this, the only poem I may write about my only sister,
I should admit nothing much has changed.
In the thirty years I've known her,
we've always been distant, estranged.

It's like I've taken a backwards somersault
and back where I stood,
I'm able to admit that visually
and emotionally, she's dead wood.

I talk to her across a divide, at the best of times.
She's the memory of a photograph I once took.
I'm sure it's nobody's fault, but I mean
like our phonecalls this needn't last hours.

Antony Nicholls

LAD'S ESTATE

The vehicle sat, one day, soft in the barn,
with whispering craneflies and fat fieldmice.
Spearmint shafts of sunlight felt us
cowering, thief-thick, quiet.
                                        Then, alarm.
Sour tomcats dodged imagined hooves,
weasel cages danced. Barn owls woke.
Calm usual crows exploded
at the motor car ignition. It shook
                all tongues and grooves.

She'd sleep beneath a canvas
                that kept the 'hen do' off.
And when we'd growled home
I'd sprawl and hear the secret random
song of cooling body parts, and cough
the petrol asking for my blood.

I'd sneak below the stiff tarpaulin,
taste the shellac varnish of her wing,
climb the ashwood ladder of her side,
lay up on her silken roof.
                                        And dream.

Philip Burton

Rejoinees

We ran our childhoods wild together;
rebellious, teasing little rascals, spent
a dozen winters under common roofs -
as many summers over common yards.

Then came the day our pal-ship waned
until it seemed it was gone.
Our gang of two disbanded,
though the thread has never broken.

Now that our roads have crossed again -
with in between your seven years
in the Peruvian Andes caring for
the poorest and mine advising

the richest how to grow richer - I
would like our trades to be as one.
I wish we could retrieve that bit
of us we discarded in the past,

resume some common habits, drink a toast
on what we were, we are, we'll be. Just talk,
forgive each other's having walked away -
- perhaps write down four-handed poems anew.

Alessio Zanelli

SYMBIONTS

You -

who know who I am, inside as well outside, of
which game I am a pawn, what makes me amble
as it likes, like a somnambule, what manoeuvres
me by means of invisible threads -

you -

be
my foot,
my hand,
my mouth.

You -
who can spot where every wobbly, erratic
step of mine alights, envision where the next
one is likely to fall, make your own way, act
and speak of our own accord -

you -

be
my spoor,
my tirade,
my invective.

You -

who can penetrate all this, as in perfect
symbiosis, throughout aware -

be
just me,
all me.
You -

have no scruples, drain my life-force and
burn away my whole caged anger -

if you really can't cut those threads.

Alessio Zanelli

It will be a good harvest

STONES

1.

Above many of the towns are
boulders that inspire a mystical awareness,
touchstones to another state of being
beneath the stars, or in the sun
with heather blooming.
But few look up and fewer climb
out of Cough Valley or Carcinogen Clough.

Though when trying to forge one truth -
to integrate the wandering spirit -
this is the place to be, where anchoring the skies
has hardly marked them and they bear
names of myths and archetypes,
Ludd's or Saint Bride's stones.

2.

Leave an indoor life caught on hooks
and the phone that threatens to ring.
Find self: a spring bubbling, clearing
its way through frozen water.

Or is 'self' an old, paved way
for sturdy packhorses, lying
in a straight line over the hills,
still, though under the grass?

Glyn Hughes

Reflections On Youth

I

It is noon, and gazing north from
my rented room, along the arc of
Bondi's famous esplanade and beach,
towards the outcrop of rock locally
known as Ben Buckler, shimmering
in the heat haze beneath a topless sky,
the yellow sand spreads like molten
butter, into the surf, as if on rye.

II

Customers saunter in and out of cafes
in a steady lunch-time trade
while giggling girls play tip-and-run
as they flirt with boys in the shade.
Brown, young, swim-suited bodies —
and some which are not so nubile are —
sprawled on their Technicolour towels,
as though posing for a Ken Done painting
or, for the more morbidly minded,
laid out like cadavers on
multi-coloured mortuary slabs.

III

Even the sunshine seems slothful.
The holiday-makers — and those who simply
have time to kill on their hands —
are aimlessly wandering; window shopping,
feeding sea-gulls; a surfeit of indolence
that prompts pondering on the adage
'youth is wasted on the young'.

IV

In the late afternoon, the sinking sun's rays
strike the windows of the apartment buildings
and deflect onto the sea, causing reflections
to bob about like globules of mercury on the water.
Then, as Sol sets behind huge banks of billowing
Cloud, the panes of glass flash orange-fire,
burning buildings in an orgy of imaginary mass destruction...

V

Night has now cast its cloak along the shore
and the lights of the Telecom telephone booth
domes are glowing like lit coals in a grate.
Fairy lights outline the silhouette of the tower
of the Bondi Hotel and the headlights of cars
search along Campbell Parade as, like whores
winking back at them, traffic lights blink red.
In the street below, buses' air-brakes hiss
as they stop to let off workers on their
way home — and the sudden wail of an
ambulance siren, demanding right of way,
sends a chill down the length of my spine.

VI

And I decide: youth isn't wasted on the young.
It is a gift, given to those in their physical
prime while they still believe they are immortal;
while the vagaries of aging are still merely mythology;
so that young years can be enjoyed without glancing
over shoulders at lengthening shadows...

Jeremy Gadd

December Garden

I went out into the snow-bright garden
to look for her.
She wasn't among the shivering goldenrod
the flimsied cone-flowers,
not hiding behind mock-orange
or weigelias, as one might have thought.
She'd left no footprints on the crazy paths,
no brushed, loose flakes
to show that she had passed.

I found a heap of bones
dropped by the lily pond,
its empty surface scrimmed with ice.
We'd put skin upon these bones
in early spring, in summer
and at the start of fall;
but now they're bare
and brittle as the frost.

Perhaps I'll bury them,
these bones, this skull,
leave them to the winter's
slow dark labour
and hope that in the spring
a creature might break through
rejuvenated, radiant.

But, I know myself
these bones cannot lie idle:
she and I together must reknit them,
pull sustenance from the hard,
unyielding ground,
from bits of mist, of trailing light,
such droppings as birds find,
to form a shape that
roots again in my mind's bed,
and blooms in its own good time.

Lucy Brennan

UNDRESSED

He has come again -
turns up one Tuesday
after a whole year
of my standing,
rooted to the spot,
waiting and waving.

I can't help myself -
I do not resist his breezy kisses,
find myself delirious,
blushing red and jaundice
while he blows away my clothes,
tickling the hollows of my body,
leaving me naked and expectant.
My robes fall to the ground,
they gossip and chatter and shrivel.

Then he's gone again -
I've lost him to the frost,
and I stand here,
bereft and nodding,
calling his name,
saying it over and over
as if to keep him close,
while the squirrels
tickle my trunk.

Miles Salter

The Lemon Tree

From Machado's 'El limonero lánguido suspende...'
The poet visits his childhood house in Seville and in due course remembers an evening similar to the present when he plunged his hands into the water of the fountain believing the lemons reflected on the surface were really lying in the water. He seems to recover a lost innocence.

The lemon tree is listlessly trailing
A pale, greying bough
Over the clear, spellbound fountain.
And there, deep down in the water,
Lie dreaming the golden lemons...
It is a bright evening
Not quite spring time,
A mild March evening
Bringing with it a breath of almost April.
And I'm standing alone in the silent patio
Trying to recall some old and childish fantasy:
Over the white-washed wall, a fleeting shadow;
On the brink of the basin, a dormant memory;
Or the train of a skirt gliding by.

Hovering in the evening air there is an awareness
Of something missing,
Something saying to the lucid mind, 'Never',
And to the heart, 'Wait'.

Something kindling the memory
Of lost and primeval fragrances.
Yes, now I remember you, bright and happy evening
Not quite springtime,
Evening not yet in bloom
Brimming over with the friendly smell of mint and basil
Growing in my mother's pots.

And so you watched me plunging my innocent hands
Into the calm water
Reaching out to the spellbound lemons
That even now lie dreaming in the fountain.

Yes, now I recognise you, bright and happy evening,
Not quite spring time.

Gloria Moreno-Castillo

ODESSA MAMA

odessa mama
i will have to leave
your pink and blue lullaby
in the morning

i shall no longer see you
shaking your fine treehair
or hear the sweeping
of your morning brushes

odessa mama
your grey cat pads across
the patterned streets
into the dried turfs of spring

odessa mama
forgive me — for I brought
stale bread to your table
i did not bring your other
daughter to you

she did not listen
to your doves
cooing reconciliation
and your trams
clearing their throats

she did not walk
in your sweet stroll
or touch your clear pearl skin

she did not watch you
on this wide green bench
curling arms nursing chatter

odessa mama
i leave without gifting you
with my heart song

how can I let you go now
as your windpalm
strokes my cheek goodbye

Note: Odessa Mama is the name all Russians have for their beautiful port.

Julia Davis

Vamp

Before a family sing-song
I heard my Uncle George whisper,
'She can't play, you know.
All she can do is vamp'.

A cohort of substantial aunts
advanced on the piano,
while Great Aunt Maud
began to play
Love's Old Sweet Song.

Half their height,
I glimpsed through a gap
her nodding Marcel wave
and plump ringed fingers
beating the time
on yellow keys.

'Vamp' I wondered, remembering
old posters at the Electric,
Theda Bara with hooded eyes
and pencilled brows.
Kiss me Again,
Come to my *Forbidden Paradise,*
she called from desert tent
and curtained couch.

And I peered again
through ample thighs,
puzzled, as Great Aunt Maud,
with wobbling forearms
and double chin
battled with
The White Cliffs of Dover.

Brian Biddle

Transcendent

Up from the deep, a roar fills the room.
Water streams down the glass.
Getting a fix on the place, eyes full of sleep,
is like swimming underwater. I don't recall checking in.

Down south, at this hour, I'd've picked out the coveralls
smeary with grease, slung over the chair;
steel-toed boots and a toolbox.
Now, up on one elbow, panning the space,
up floats the proof of last night —
blue dress and heels, punk-rocker's wig;
stubs in the ashtray, kissed with wet lipstick.

For a change, I take my time dressing.
Smile at the mirror. Totter carefully down
to the gallery, stand in the mist of the Falls:
sodden without, glowing within
at each stolen glance —
faced as we are with such wonder —
blue clinging tight to my skin.

André Mangeot

The Manhattan Skyline and Radio 4

You will say our first hello in April at the crossroads.
You'll sit on a green bench at the memorial inspecting
my Spanish guitar. Wind will lift the dust and snow will follow.

How often we will sit in your mother-dusted front room.
You will finger-pick *Angie*, jaunty folk-song masterpiece,
like the real, legendary Bert Jansch. I will be entertained.

Your parents will be behind the kitchen door. Kitchen duty
and DIY. They will die aged 55 and 64. Heart trouble.
You will not become a legendary Jansch or Robert Johnson.

You'll do other things. You'll walk the streets of Manhattan
sixteen hours a day. Your leg muscles will grow tough.
You will shoot from various angles the gaps in the skyline.

You'll shoot walls. You'll send condolences. It will be April.
You'll tell me again about the walls in your life, the gaps
aged 55 and 64. Kitchen duty and DIY. The heart's rubble.

You will tell me you have stopped smoking, really.
You'll want to go home. It will still be April.
I'll imagine you will see a red sunset, Manhattan dust.

This will be part of the evidence, the archaeological record.
After the dinosaurs, several black clouds will circle the planet.
There'll be bridges, shipyards and utilities. There'll be legends.

My Spanish guitar will circle the planet. My big-hearted dad
will circle the planet and your parents will circle the planet.
They'll be part of the dust of Manhattan and the snow.

Once, I'll be telling someone close what you did and said.
Angie will be playing in the background. Radio 4 will tell me:
You'll meet in April at a crossroads. Dust and snow will follow.

Philip Foster

FOOTBRIDGE

'Look, now we have turned, do you see how
vee frames of the bridge cast their shadow
echoingly faint on the far side's
wire-lattice, but skewed by the angle?

'How often we've taken our walk here
nor seen in the odd burst of sunshine
that delicate cross-hatch of shading.
Now when there's a chance we will spot it.'

— One day here our last walk together.
Then, oh, then may nothing noteworthy
way-mark any point in the mind's eye.
Like most of the rest strolled as usual. —

'"Robin Hoodlum Turney." Remember?
That redbreast we saw fight his rival,
outfaced by a dumped rear-view mirror.
We'll call today, "Shadow Bridge Saunter".'

Peter Dale

Natural Worlds
for Clea

Like being fluent in both tongues...

Not confluent:
                                    the lick and purl
and play in you of each describes

a sweet excess words
can't contain, un-
translatable into the other... At
home in either
                                    differently

as the dolphin

not by cruel
instruction   but by

her very nature is

in the company of man and of her own kind.

Tony Flynn

Lanterns for the Dead

The Moon has waxed to a perfect round. It gazes
on the lantern festivities down below. Every inch

of the land is ablaze with millions of lights, as if
the earth itself is on fire. Everyone is on the move to

arrive home when the Moon is seen in its thinnest sliver,
the first day of the Lunar New Year. For fourteen

days, each stage of the waxing orb is celebrated,
waiting for its final fullness when round lanterns

are lit and raised for family reunion, including ancestors,
recent and remote. All gaps close; three circles complete.

Lanterns are placed all the way to graveyards, lighting
the paths for the dead to find their way back home.

But the dead who are turned into ashes, what paths can be
lit for them? How will the spirits find their way back?

In a foreign land, I light a lantern, hang it
in the doorway, sit and wait for my mother.

Rani Drew

The Invisible Child - An Autobiography *by Joolz Denby*

Introduction

It's the twenty-ninth of November 1997. I'm forty-two years of age, and I'm tired. Not an auspicious start to a memoir, some would say, but then, they haven't had my life. I think I was about eleven when the full horror of what was going to be expected of me began to dawn - at any rate it was around the start of puberty. I do recall I'd been grievously lied to about menstruation. I believed it would only last a day, if that, and the terrible combination of blood, pain and Mother and Nana dismissing my sobs of disbelief and panic with strangely satisfied expressions as they told me it would last a week, was a nightmare I couldn't escape. A week! It wasn't possible that ferocious Indian Brave, Red Feather (me) would have to put up with this squalid and hurtful indignity every month, for a week, *forever*. It was disgusting. It was a betrayal. Worse still, all these women were gloating over me with I-told-you-so expressions. Red Feather was dead, those faces said, and now I'd have to buckle down and be a girl.

I was a child, but I wasn't stupid.

There was a bottomless pit of humiliation opening up in front of me, and those women seemed to expect I'd jump into it singing 'All Things Bright and Beautiful'. Maybe it was then I decide to live my life at a full tilt boogie and damn gender.

But perhaps it wasn't ever a conscious decision and all I've done is hurtle from one crisis to another, to avoid that yawning pit. It's said we all perish from our own rage - and that we always meet what we fear the most. Well then, at some point I looked fury dead in the eye and hooked a bridle on it. It's been a bumpy ride, me buckos.

PART ONE

Chapter 1

I expect you'll be relieved to know I don't have many memories of being very little. I often speak to people who claim to have almost total recall of their toddling days and eulogise their Teddies as if they were dead siblings. I have always suspected that for recall of that clarity, you need the co-operation of your family. *Mummy says I was a terror aged two* and *remember when I bit the cat - my, how we laughed*, that kind of thing. It seems to me to be a collective, rather than a personal memory. In my family, the past was a dark and dangerous voyage that had been successfully navigated to the present and what was the point of talking about it? My parents specialise in deleting what was, editing memory and denying the rest. So, a minimum of cutesy baby snaps, just the photos of me on a white fur rug - nude, except for my baby bangles (nothing changes), in a square necked frock and pearls looking plumply fractious, with Nana's dog, Senta, faithfully guarding me in my pram. I don't really remember these things, I just look at the photos and seem to feel Senta's dark, rough coat, or smell . . . What? Nothing, to be honest. I was a *baby*, born in a hot April in 1955, the year Bill Haley released 'Rock Around the Clock'.

The birth took place in Colchester Barracks (or more properly, the Officer's Quarters) where Father was stationed, at around two a.m. Some mythology surrounds my entrance into the world; it was a home birth and apparently, though I have no idea if it's actually true, the bed props collapsed during the last moments of Mother's labour, the resultant crash summoned Father from the sitting room where he had been nursing a bottle of whiskey, and the sight of this bloody confusion caused him to faint dead away. At six foot four inches and a bit tall, this must have been like watching a great tree being felled in the forest. Mother noticed none of this, having demanded gas-and-air at the first contraction and so having been off with the pixies for several hours, where some would say, she has remained. I always sensed from this story that I was an ungrateful baby, since it was generally prefaced by Mother's saying what a good prenatal carer she'd been, having given up cigarettes at the first hormonal flood (though she lit up immediately after the placenta popped out and never looked back) for Jaffa oranges, with which she stuffed herself for the remainder of the pregnancy. Her Siamese cat, Gina

Lollobridgida, would sit purring on the vast dome of Mother's belly for hours, offering some sort of feline lullaby as I swam in the warmth and safety of that orange-flavoured amniotic fluid. The other comment that made me aware I'd caused difficulty was Mother's assertion that it had taken a full six months of sit-ups for her to regain her famously svelte figure. That, I still feel, was in many ways my gravest crime.

About two months after my nerve-wracking entrance to the world, Father left the Army - he said it was because he felt promotion from Captain upwards would be too long coming, a case of stepping into dead men's shoes. Maybe so. But there were other forces at work; Mother craved the worldly sophistication of civvie life - the cocktail parties, or costume dances where she would appear as a smouldering, glossy-lipped Flamenco dancer, or saucy 'Cherry Ripe' (her name is Cherrie - actually, Cherrie Joyce but the 'Joyce', considered a tad common, is never mentioned; Nana very nearly called her 'Blossom' apparently so things could have been worse) in a little black dress and a bunch of imitation cherries and net by way of a hat. Matching lips and nails in brilliant crimson naturally completed the effect.

Mother *was* Glamour. She wanted more than the hermetic, deadly world of Army Wives. We moved in with my Grandparents, at their end-of-terrace house on Hawthorn Crescent, Cosham, near Portsmouth. I have no idea how my Grandparents came to be in Portsmouth - was it something to do with my Grandfather? Like Father, he'd been a career soldier; after retirement, mysteriously, he'd moved his family to this anonymous, undistinguished suburb of Pompey - a famous Navy town. We had no other relatives either there or nearby; had the sea drawn him? Was it purely financial? I don't know. It was a snug house though, and the walled garden was a sleepy sun-trap. 1955 had seen a hot spring and it turned into a very hot summer; I was put out in the sun, naked, a minute on each side, because that was the healthy thing to do then, before melanoma and Factor 60. Let the baby get the air, a bit of sunshine puts roses in your cheeks. I got so tanned, and my thick cap of hair was so dark, when I was wheeled out in my pram, strangers told Mother she was really brave to adopt a black baby. Mother, naturally, like the good bigot she is, was horrified at the idea people would think that of her. It was just another proof of my ability to annoy her.

Was I a 'good' baby? Is anyone? What does that mean anyway - that you don't give any trouble by crying or getting sick? I don't know. I do know that my maternal Grandfather, the extremely troublesome William Edward (or Edwin, according to some accounts) George Hurdle, was apparently the only adult in the house who could calm me when I did cry. That Mother couldn't, is, in her eyes, yet another testament to my intractability. Can you see how this is shaping? I couldn't. I thought Mother was a Beautiful Fairy Princess; I thought I simply wasn't good enough for her. I'm sure I felt it even then. Is this why I cried and cried until my Grandfather took me in his arms and soothed me back to sleep?

Bill Hurdle is a strange, enigmatic figure. I feel a curious tenderness towards this man I never knew, and who by all accounts was a terrible person. I've very often been described as that myself so maybe a little bias creeps in. He was supposedly a strict, tyrannical martinet, a manic-depressive, given massive doses of ECT, who once chased Nana round the garage with an axe and whose Mother died of 'galloping consumption' after going to a dance in rural County Clare with another man and after he abandoned her, getting soaking wet walking home afterwards in her dancing slippers. From this, by the way, Nana extrapolated that I was a potential TB victim, and set in motion my long love-affair with disease – but more of that later.

Bill Hurdle, or 'Weg' Hurdle as I call him to myself, after the initials stencilled on his Army issue tin box which I still have, had been part of the teams that went round the villages surrounding the concentration camps after the War, taking depositions from the inhabitants.

'Did you see anything?' he'd ask the stolid German burghers, 'did you know what was happening - the black smoke, the stench, didn't you know what it was?'

They always said no. Always. Despite the fact you could still smell the stink of the ovens as they stood and denied everything. It maddened him. I think it destroyed him.

But despite his ruined spirit, he loved me. I was the child of his heart.

If I woke in the night crying, my Grandfather would carry me round in his arms until I quietened, talking to me in a low voice, telling me things that sank into my brain like ink on a piece of blotting paper. Telling me things that left their bloody, formless stain on my soul; walking round and round his room with me while the disturbing moon outside stirred our blood to boiling point. Do I feel connected to him because I share his violent heritage - perhaps. The things our ancestors bequeath us are not as easily explained as we might like to believe. I don't look like him, though; in the photographs he appears spare and almost gaunt, with hollow eyes, a haunted expression and a brutal military haircut. His ears stick out; mine are small and neat, despite now being so heavily pierced. But I see a certain look in his eyes, in those monochrome pictures. It's a look I've seen in the mirror - it says, I don't know if I can survive this day of inane, human chatter and the vast desolation that is eating my heart; it says, Goddess forgive me and have mercy on my pain; it says, *release* me.

Even his humour was manic, hysterical, gasping - the photo of him imitating a cobra being charmed by his friend playing a recorder, which involved him lying on the floor face down with a jacket over his head and one arm bent up, hand bunched into a snake's head, reeks of that high, unstoppable craziness that I hear in my own voice, drunk and on overload.

Then he died.

Nana believed it was because she had brought snowdrops into the house. It was a superstition in her Mother's family; snowdrops should never be brought inside because if they were, someone would die. The Fairies didn't like their favourite flower being killed just to decorate human houses with their pretty corpses; they took revenge. A human life for a flower's life - it's all the same to the Little Folk. But that day, someone had given Nana a bunch and she hadn't wanted to cause offence by refusing to cross the threshold with them. Perhaps she wanted to shake off the dark, Welsh peasant heritage that would have seemed primitive and rather shameful to her - for whatever reason, she broke the superstition of her Mother's people and brought the little white flowers in. That night my Grandfather suffered a massive coronary and died. He died before I knew him, my protector died, and from then on, it was save yourself and the devil take the hindmost.

I don't remember much after this for a few years - I suppose it was a house in mourning but I was too little to understand, even if I felt it. Then, when I was a toddler, Mother's brother, Uncle Tom, a person I have no memory of ever seeing or hearing about previous to his death, died in Aden, where he'd been stationed with the RAF. Actually, he died in England having been flown home after having a brain haemorrhage whilst playing water-polo. At the approximate time of his seizure, Nana had again taken snowdrops into the house; a world away, her son began his dying.

It was like a fate, or a terrible curse; as if the narrow Welsh valley she'd abandoned reached out and claimed her men as its price for her betrayal. The house grew dark and cold; voices never raised above a whisper. Uncle Tom's widow, Auntie Peggy, and her two adolescent daughters, Pattie and Cherry (Mother's namesake) came to live with us. It was a confused time for me; I have a vague recollection of a busybody neighbour saying to Nana in the street, *does the little one know, 'ave you told her, poor mite?* It made Nana angry and I was puzzled - what had happened? Who was 'Uncle Tom'? Why were these strange women coming to live with us? Why did grown-ups cry all the time and get furious when you asked what the matter was? I was terrified of my cousins, especially Pattie, who was sharp and hateful with grief, taking her anger out on me, who to her, must have seemed to be a spoilt brat with no notion of how cruel life could be. She set out to show me, in little ways, what a mean place the world could be, when the adults weren't around.

So it was a house of dying. I was born into mourning and tears, inheriting my Grandfather's black humours and his clever hands, the hands that made intricate model galleons and mended watches, the artist's eyes that filled exquisite handmade leather albums with hundreds of beautiful photographs of his travels, that tumultuous heart that finally burst.

So it was that my whole family, a family of women with one man, my Father, came to live in Nana's house, settling there like a harem of crows.

Chapter 2

A child growing up in Cosham learns about the sea in a different way to a child who has a two week holiday a year at a resort. Nana once told me that the seagulls who wheeled above our heads cawing mournfully were the souls of dead sailors drowned at sea. She was prone to that kind of lugubrious superstition: she also said if you stepped on a needle it would get into your body, then travel round your blood stream until it pierced your heart, that pins carried a mysterious poison called 'verdygris' and raw cake mix gave you worms. However, if the seagulls thing sounds a bit nautical, a bit sea-doggish, it wasn't, because Cosham is on the mainland, Portsmouth City is an island,

and they're separated by a saltwater creek, deep and muddy, reeking of decay and silt. I believe its been filled in now, which is a great shame because I loved it and my childhood was spent secretly prowling its banks looking for dead things to prod at.

Naturally, as a child my life centred around the house most of the time, and I played in the garden, the alley and the street. Excursions to the creek were carried out undercover of supposed nippings round to the sweetie shop, or the park or whatever. The creek, or more precisely, the grassy unkempt creek-bank, was dangerous, an outlaw place where my friends and I built dens out of branches and seaweed; iodine rich and womb-like. These dens were often vandalised or desecrated by strangers in the night; we'd find beer bottles, empty cigarette cartons and once, a vast, primeval human turd. We fished for flatfish with bits of yellow car sponge on bent pins - sometimes sacrificing Opal Fruits, as fish were supposed to be partial to them, if you chewed them for a while first. I never caught anything so I never found out what flavour they like best.

One reason I liked wandering round the creek bank was that Home was still pretty fraught with problems. I had grown used to the presence of my Aunt and cousins and become quite fond of Cousin Cherry, who was arty and drew me pictures of horses galloping madly into nothing (scenery was not included.) The days were easily filled with whatever it is that children do in their internal world - it must have included drawing and reading of some sort because I can't remember learning to read or for that matter, to swim. I can't remember a time when I couldn't do either of those two things well. I do remember eating plastic beads (tiny little multi-coloured ones used for bead weaving) from little plastic bags; they were kept in the old kitchen cupboard, (the one near the door, with a top covered in yellow sticky backed plastic that had bubbled up and gone villainously black at the ratty edges), for some reason, though no one did craft-work to my knowledge. I savoured their texture, like taramasalata without the fish grease; bumpy, delicious. They didn't taste of anything but I loved how they felt. Eventually I was caught engaging in this illegal snacking and the dreadful word SCHOOL was mentioned, striking terror into my heart. I was at nursery school already because Mother worked at the Electricity Board being smart and glam as a typist (though she was really a secretary, she said, adding to the impression she was a Princess in Disguise, forced to labour in circumstances below her dignity) in a typing pool - a workplace that has mystified the children of its workers on many occasions. My vision of it was a kind of Fifties mermaid factory, in which Mother and her equally soigné chums typed and floated in a cool, turquoise light spangled with glitter.

I don't remember Father being around - perhaps he was working in the Persian Gulf at that point. Then, though I don't remember a homecoming or anything, he was suddenly *there*, enormous and rough-chinned, smelling of Old Spice and all the women treated him like an exotic creature who's every whim must be catered to with a resigned sigh.

'Ronnie wants a bath, Mum, shall I put the heater on in the bathroom?'

'Well, I should think so - unless we've run out of paraffin - get it nice and snug.'

Father's constant complaint was that above the tiny bath in the midget bathroom were strung thin plastic indoor washing lines that came complete with miniature plastic pegs, and on these lines were draped 'smalls' that had been hand washed - knickers, stockings, bras - and they dripped on him as he tried to bathe, dribbling cold drips on his head and down his neck. The bathroom heater was lit in order to fool him with heat, so he wouldn't notice that chilly shower. The heater itself was a vile, smelly brute of a thing, ancient and malevolent as only certain household devices can be. It burnt my bum once when I inadvertently backed into it and Nana sprinkled the burn with a mysterious silver powder from a small rusty tin, a leftover from her days in Germany. I have no idea what it was, but it worked miraculously.

While this house of women revolved round Father - huge and handsome - I attended my nursery school and pondered the strangeness of other children as only children often do. Other children seemed remote, alien, unfriendly, and even then, dull and conservative. For example, when the school tortoise pissed on the table, its opalescent, milky urine fascinated me; I felt suddenly that it was possible other things, other creatures, other people even, could be different from me, have different existences. That there were an infinite number of variations, individual stories of creation, of life. Not, of course, that I could say that, being four years old or thereabouts. But as I turned, mouth agape with wonder, to the teacher, about to ask a stream of questions, I froze at the scarlet-cheeked evidence of her embarrassment and the scatological sniggerings of my classmates. I felt the world zoom away for an instance and a terrible feeling of loneliness drenched me and instead of questions, I cried out in horror. This was taken as 'soppiness' by teacher and peer-group alike and Mother was told, when she collected me, I was 'over-sensitive' or worse, had an 'over developed imagination'.

On another occasion, everyone in class had to sing a song, so as to earn a couple of squares of Kake-Brand cooking chocolate. They sang hymns, children's songs, nursery rhymes. I sang 'My Old Man's A Dustman', by Lonny Donegan, the Skiffle King. I have absolutely no idea where I learnt it, but I knew off by heart and sang away happily not realising the silence was not admiration of my vocalising, but incredulity. I faltered to a stop, thinking my singing was so terrible I wouldn't get the chocolate, which I badly wanted. It was from this incident my love of singing was first sabotaged by the idea I was the world's worst singer, ever. I must have cried, because I always cried, hot and humiliated.

I don't remember if I got the chocolate, but I probably did as I remember clearly the thick, waxy taste of it, so unlike real chocolate. Mother was again informed of my oddness, and this time she was also mortified by my vulgarity. I only made up for it by reciting 'The Owl And The Pussycat' faultlessly at the nursery school Fête, but even then I lost points for stoutly refusing to take off a particularly disreputable beanie hat I loved to distraction. It didn't *go* with my frilly white dress and immaculate rag rolled Shirley Temple curls. Mother and Nana loved those long, shining sausage curls and I suffered agonies because of them; I didn't want curls, I loathed curls and my hair is naturally thick, straight and deeply resistant to curling. But what could I do? If a grown woman wants to bind a child's long hair up into tight, painful bumps of cloth and make her sleep like that, there's not much a child can do - and anyhow, it was something that girls had to do, we had to 'suffer to be beautiful' like that foul song 'Keep Young And Beautiful':

Keep young and beautiful,
It's your duty to be beautiful!
Keep young and beautiful,
If you want to be loved.

Jesus Christ, how sinister is that? But it was the motivating ethos of our house and I wasn't going to escape it. Is it any wonder I longed passionately to be a boy?

I remember night times best. Nana's front room was always a warm, glowing place, wrapped in the blasting heat of the coal fire and gilded by the glow of the standard lamp behind the comfortable, saggy old sofa where I always sat. The TV would be on, Nana, Mother and Auntie Peggy would be drinking Merrydown cider and sometimes, daringly, (from a perpetual dieter's point of view), eating bacon-and-egg sandwiches instead of a proper dinner. Sometimes there was gin-and-tonics, which was a red letter day. They would drink and smoke Embassys and I would read, goggle at the telly or roam about the room, investigating the old writing desk where Auntie Peggy kept her nail varnish - 'Orange Flip' - and Mother's - 'Rose Frosted Rose Gold', by Revlon. The smell of nail polish and the old leather writing surface blended in a secret, intoxicating aroma.

Behind the sofa was a cold, outcast place, taken up by a lonely, unused armchair and the glass-fronted cabinet containing treasures from the family's Army life, a life which had allowed them to travel extensively. They had lived in Egypt for a short time and for a long time in Germany; Nana spoke wistfully of the souvenirs that had fallen by the way in their journeys - the trunk full of ostrich feathers devoured by the mysterious and voracious 'woolly bear bug', a waist length string of carved ivory beads the size of walnuts Mother had played with and broken, the beads scattering and never recovered. But the cabinet was a nest of wonders to me, even if to Nana it was a poor shadow of former glories.

On the top stood elaborate, carved and painted musical beer Steins, a wooden bear, a painted, wooden Smoking Man incense burner - when the incense cone was lit and the figure re-assembled, smoke poured out of his mouth as if he'd lit his pipe. I still have him, he still smokes. There was a beautiful porcelain statue of a rosy naked lady, an exquisite model schooner in full sail made by Grandfather and a brass ashtray of the Manikin GIs urinating on a swastika, from Belgium. Inside was full of things like the little clay oil lamp supposedly from the Valley Of The Kings and an oval Ormolu box inlaid with gemstones, a 'real' diamond twinkling dustily on its lid. Best of all, there was a wooden musical box carved with edelweiss that creaked out an asthmatic waltz - I loved it so much it made me cry. I still get tearful listening to musical boxes, they seem so plucky and desperate, like an asthmatic street singer on a frosty evening.

Sometimes, tired out with examining these domestic ikons, I would just sit in the curve of the sofa and watch Nana sitting opposite me with her little mongrel dog Sally tucked in beside her - Senta, my faithful black guard dog, who had been half Alsatian and half Labrador and who had been brought home from Germany despite the trouble of quarantine, was long dead and presumably in Dog Heaven. Sally, a little neurotic, pop-eyed groveller had been acquired because apparently, I had become frightened of big dogs and Sally's hysterical angst was supposed to re-assure me dogs were Alright. Personally, I think anyone who isn't at least a little bit frightened of big dogs wants their head examining - have you actually looked at those *teeth?*

If I tired of gazing at Nana, there was always Auntie Peggy fascinatingly knitting Fair Isle, reading and watching TV all at the same time. If Mother was there, and not out with Father, I'd watch her more covertly, admiring her beauty and her soft turquoise eye-shadow, which I thought was a natural skin colouration that happened to women as they grew up; Auntie Peggy had it too, and so did Nana which proved my theory, but I was too young to realise they shared the pot of Max Factor Cream Eyeshadow in Seagreen. If I got too hot, I'd slide over to the parquet flooring by the bay window and lie on the cool, shiny wood, breathing the scent of cold and floor polish in a doze of pleasure.

This habit earned me a slap round the face from Pattie once when she was forced to baby-sit one night. I was astonished and outraged at the injustice but to her, my indignation was doubtless the result of my spoilt nature. I'd probably disobeyed her, something she very much disliked in anyone. She was very tall and willowy, and had fabulous big hairdos courtesy of being a hairdressers model - often these beehives were tinted pastel green or pink, very chic, with nails by Mavala to match. Her beautiful net petticoats, layers and layers of sugar-water stiffened multicoloured net, pushed her skirts out in a crinoline and her shoes were evilly pointed. We never got on. I did admire one of her boyfriends though, a boy called Malcolm, who built Lego castles for me and on one occasion, helped me to be brave.

I had crashed my bicycle in the alley and gone over the handlebars into a pothole fracturing three or four ribs. In those days, the Doctors bound you up from nipple to waist in thick white Elastoplast strapping to prevent your breathing too heavily. The time came to remove this sticky corset and chaos reigned. Mother tried inching off a bit at a time, but my screams threatened to bring the Police on a child battering call. I was bribed (with chocolate, naturally), threatened, cajoled - everything. By the time Pattie and Malcolm got in, things were desperate and I was in full mutiny. I'd live with the plaster for the rest of my life if need be, rather than go through the slow torture of its removal. Malcolm (to Pattie's disgust) knelt down to me and solemnly asked me if I would be a good soldier and let him rip it off in one pull. It would hurt, he said, but be over quickly. I couldn't let him down, I'd have died for him, never mind let him rip my plaster off. I agreed. He did it. It burnt like fire but the look of admiration on his face was the reward of heaven. I prayed nightly that Pattie would marry him so he'd be mine forever and of course, come and live in the house, which is how I thought life was lived. But she didn't, and shortly afterwards, my Knight in Shining Armour was an ex. And I never saw him again. Lego lost its appeal.

Cherry on the hand, kept rabbits and mice which was quite nice, though I never had much to do with them. She was a terrific Mod, in grey flannel pinafore dresses, black polo-neck jumpers and, thrillingly, black leather boots with a seam up the front. Her boyfriends rode scooters and were knife-sharp. She was an Art Student and tremendously cool, with short, Quant-style hair. Nana queued up for hours to get her a ticket to see the Beatles when they came to the Guildhall. Cherry studied Window Dressing, and made fascinating things out of papier maché. I wanted to be close to her, but though she was the younger of the girls, she was too old to care about a child other than the occasional kindness. My cousins and I were never 'sisters', never close in any way. We just lived in the same house for a while; I seldom ever saw them after we left, or indeed to this day. It reinforced my feeling that families consisted of people who were unfortunately related, but existed in a sort of bubble with no past, no joint future and no real connection to each other apart from the accident of birth. I was still an only child, and though the girls adored Father and co-opted him as best they could, it didn't make me part of their lives.

Nana was the central figure in my childhood. I lived in her house and she looked after me while Mother worked - some very stupid people would say that this deprivation caused all my problems. As if it were that easy. Nana was a quiet, wrinkly apple of a woman who taught me how to carry my doll Patsy, (she was a yellowy pink, leprous creature with a terrifying bald, battered celluloid head and a greying rubber body - I ate her fingers and toes in a cannibalistic frenzy when I was forbidden the beads) strapped to my hip by means of a shawl tied diagonally across to the opposite shoulder. This was how her Mother carried babies in Crumlin, the village in Wales Nana had come from - Lily May Burgess from Crumlin, though she thought 'Lilian' a more up-market name and tended to use that instead.

My Great-Grandmother figured quite largely in my imagination at this time. Although not at all forthcoming about her life, like all my family, Nana did sometimes mention her childhood in Wales when we were alone. My Great-Grandparents had lived in a steep sided mining village in a two up, two down cottage which was unusual, but my Great-Grandfather had worked his way up to becoming a mines inspector, and so took home more money than average. Which was just as well, because they had sixteen children, many of whom were twins, and fourteen of whom were boys, Nana and her sister being the exceptions. Nana told me her Mother put up two pillowcases of dough every Monday, and took them to the village bakehouse to be baked into quartain loaves for the week. The family was never all in the house at the same time - especially when the boys went down the pit on shift.

I used to ponder this excess of brothers for hours, as I longed desperately for a brother of my own. It seemed fantastic, impossible - how did Great-Grandmother ever get her figure back? Nana told a couple of other stories, such as when, having daringly gone to the pictures and seen a Western, the two girls decided that Nana's sister (who's name I never knew) would become an Indian Squaw, which involved them covering her long, thick, curling auburn hair with black boot polish and braiding it tightly. Her head had to be shaved as a result. Another time, Nana dabbed her face with Papier Poudré, the little 'book' of face powder impregnated paper leaves designed to take the shine off your nose - Great-Grandfather scrubbed her face under the pump with carbolic soap for 'painting her face like a trollop'. She said his great white handlebar moustache was quivering with rage. Nana said my hands were the same shape as Great-Grandmother's, that used to make me happy, as if I really did have some connection with the past, some roots, and I used to look at my long fingers and imagine that Welsh life, that narrow valley.

But Nana never said why she left, what she did before she married Grandfather or why we had no contact whatsoever with her family. Was it a scandal, or was it more mundane, simply the search for work outside the valley, drifting away, trying to climb the social ladder? She did tell me she only married Grandfather on the rebound, having been terribly in love with a handsome tubercular (TB again, a recurring theme) boy who played the piano and died, tragically and romantically (the great myth of TB, I just cannot imagine why coughing up your lungs in bloody lumps is considered attractive). She married Grandfather because, she said, she felt sorry for him . . . Oh, Nana, where are all my Welsh relatives? Where are those curly headed boys filthy with coal dust, their white teeth gleaming as they smiled at their sister Lily? Where are my Grand-Uncles, my second cousins and second cousins twice removed? Not all dead, surely? I've never managed to find them and such is my inability to feel familial bonds, I probably wouldn't know what to do with them if I did - but I'd like to have had a chance to try.

My life was bound tightly with Nana's, like the doll-baby strapped to my side was bound to me. I breathed her smells, slept with her, lived her life, ate her food. Nana cooked the world's best cabbage - boiled vitaminless, thick with pepper and butter, mashed with the edge of a saucer in the pan to the consistency of pureé. Her chocolate sponge cakes were sandwiched with a fat layer of butter, cocoa and sugar mixed together; her Sunday dinners guaranteed to send everyone off to sleep in front of the TV Sunday Afternoon Matineé.

And yet, despite all the domesticity, the household maintenance, the cool perfection of her Nanahood, she was distant, uninvolved. There was something missing in her, she never lost her temper, never reacted, I don't remember her exhibiting any great degree of emotion. She had a phrase which she used to bring me to heel, and it never, ever failed.

'You can go off people, you know.'

'Nana, Nana, not me, not me, you couldn't go off *me*, Nana, I love you . . .'

'Well then, you'd better be a good girl, then, hadn't you?'

It terrified me, that phrase. I had nightmares about the family, individually or collectively, just turning away from me as I begged and pleaded for them to stay, to love me as I loved them - they'd turn away and say that dreadful phrase, adding, 'and we've/I've gone off *you*'. And they'd leave me, as if I was nothing, nothing to them. The worst thing was, in the dream, *I never knew what I'd done to make them go off me.* I used to scream myself awake and wet the bed. As I slept in a baby bed next to Nana's bed in her room, she'd take me in with her. If I wet her bed, she'd get up without grumbling and lay a towel under me and we'd sleep together in the piss soaked bed. I'd fall asleep wondering how long she'd put up with me for.

That bedroom was a strange place, above the living room and the same size. It smelt of face powder and old scent, the bay windows facing the street never opened. It had huge old wardrobes full of Mother's beautiful dance dresses - one I remember was a flame coloured strapless ball gown of many chiffon layers, with a ruched strapless bodice and a floating scarf attached which draped over one shoulder.

I can't express how beautiful Mother looked and how delicious she smelled as she would kiss me goodnight before going out to a 'do'. Her gleaming scarlet lips, her shining chestnut hair in elegant, convoluted waves, her huge blue eyes enhanced with mascara; no child ever had a Mother more entrancing to look at. She was far lovelier than any illustration in my books. Sometimes when I had a fever, which I did quite often due to what Nana termed my 'lungs', as if lungs were a condition rather than an organ, Mother would appear before going out in the bedroom doorway and would seem to be surrounded by a softly glowing halo of light (from the open door into the landing, no doubt) like a real, actual fairy. Diamonds (well, diamantès) glittered on her earlobes, neck, fingers and wrists. Even her strappy silver dance shoes gleamed glassily like Cinderella's slippers. And Father, too, so very handsome; tall and broad, with his hand-tailored suits, military bearing, clipped moustache, Scots burr and piercing grey eyes. They were a veritable Prince and Princess. How did they manage to spawn the Frog Child?

Because even then I knew I wouldn't *do*. Nana's distant gaze seemed to tell me I just wasn't up to scratch, not the child her beautiful daughter should have had. Now, I think Nana was a woman gutted by the deaths of her men, with nothing to live for, nothing to look forward to. In an unguarded moment Mother once let slip that Uncle Tom was the favourite and she always felt left out - now history repeated itself and she left me out; the cousins left me behind and poor Auntie Peggy was a cypher, the Widow who longed to be Merry but wasn't allowed to sully the memory of the Golden Boy.

So from an early age, I learned that if you didn't show off, you were simply ignored. That would never do because if you didn't get people's attention, you would slowly, slowly just disappear bit by bit, like Alice's Cheshire Cat, until you vanished with a faint sigh. You would become invisible, cease to exist. Possibly, years later, someone might pause, a drink halfway to their lips, wave their cigarette casually and say to their companion, *wasn't there a little girl living here, do you remember? I'm sure there was - long brown hair, rather plump, whatever happened to her?*

And no-one would know.

Chapter 3

A few things do stick in my memory from around this time. One is The Mudlark Incident. I had seen on telly a local news item about young boys called (by the media) 'Mudlarks' who jumped and cavorted around in the (stinking, fish-slimy, effluent contaminated) mud of Pompey Harbour, where haughty Sixties tourists, grinning sailors and louche locals threw coins to them in encouragement of their antics. I was thrilled, really thrilled with this idea - the fabulous possibilities associated with being covered in mud, the ruination of the hated sausage curls and the cute outfit du jour, and the potential for truly *mighty* showing off. Also there were cross gender and showbiz overtones which made it irresistible.

The following Sunday, after I had experienced my muddy epiphany, my parents were hosting one of their famous 'Brunch' parties. The house was full of cackling, braying drunks laughing hilariously at their own stupidity and being, as they fondly imagined, madly bohemian. It was perfect. I went out into the alley and found a crater full of mud. I rolled in it, wallowed in it, rubbed it in and it was, I have to say, bliss. I planned on leaping into the middle of the party with a glad cry of 'Look! I'm a *Mudlark*!' Thus becoming the centre of delighted attention and admiration for my comic brilliance and initiative. So I did it. There was a terrible silence and my capering tailed off to a disconsolate shuffle. The drunks looked at me as if I were insane. Mother looked stricken. Father's brow furrowed with distaste. I felt the tears gathering behind my rather itchy mud-rimmed eyes and my lower (mud-covered) lip began to tremble. This wasn't how it was meant to be - why weren't they all laughing and saying what a clever, funny little thing I was? Just as I started to howl, Nana whisked me off upstairs to the bathroom where I was scrubbed down hastily, probably with bleach.

Nana kept up a running commentary as she sluiced me down.

'How could you upset your Mummy like that? All those people, what will they think? What were you thinking of, you wicked girl? They'll think your Mummy's a *bad Mother.* Oh, you have let us down, showing off like that - I don't know where you get it from, I really don't . . .'

'But Nana, I was being a Mudlark, like on telly, like those boys on the telly, I was . . .'

'A *Mudlark*? Whatever next! Those nasty, dirty boys! Only bad boys from bad homes go on like that, Borstal Boys, not a nice little girl from a good, nice home. Stop crying now, it's your own fault, you brought it on yourself; you're a naughty, wilful little madam, a disgrace! Showing us all up like that . . .'

It was after this I realised I didn't see the world as the rest of my family did. Or if they did have an individual vision, they weren't letting on.

Another memory is, I think somewhat earlier - or maybe not, it's hard to pin it down. I was playing by the kerb in the street outside the house, and Nana, or Nana and Mother, were in the tiny patch of privet hedged front garden, talking either to each other or a neighbour (unusual, because we never consorted with neighbours in the general way, to the extent I never spoke to the neighbours all the time I lived in Cosham). I was in a curious, dreamy state that still occasionally comes on me, where everything is out of focus and far away and I feel free from the constraints of normal society or behaviour; it's as if I'm not fully awake, but I am. As I played mindlessly at something, I tripped and rolled into the road. Time stood still. A truck was barrelling down the street towards me. I was paralysed with fear, I couldn't move or scream as the howling, screeching machine bore down on me. I dimly felt Nana, or Mother, running towards me screaming but it all seemed far, far away and unconnected to me. I knew I was going to die, horribly. It seemed natural, didn't everyone die in my house? I let go of the world. I went back into my head. Then, suddenly it was all bright and fast as a hand grabbed me and pulled me back onto the pavement. Of course, I burst into tears; so did Mother and Nana, we cried and they scolded me soundly for frightening them. But something important had happened. I knew I was mortal; that life was finite - that one day I, yes, even I, would die and it would be the end. No soppy Sunday School Heaven, no harp and angel wings, no white floppy frock. And also, no Devil, no flames of Hell, no savage Christian torture garden, no retribution - only what we had in our own heads. That sense of mortality has never left me. Life is like an endless school summer holiday with Death as the First Day Back, it overshadows every pleasure, every entertainment, you know there's no escape. I think it became increasingly difficult to discipline me in the usual, physical manner after that, and they had to resort to more subtle, lasting, psychological means to control me.

Around this time, I had a friend, which was unusual for me, I was never big on friends, especially female ones. Girls always seemed so sly and treacherous, they were strong and savage but covered it up with pouts and sobs and sticky, cutesy-pie pretends. As Red Feather, I was above such behaviour, the honour of the tribe depended on my pride and considerable dead-eye prowess with the spud gun and bow and sucker-arrows. Sad, really, because I was, and still am, a terrible physical coward and had to bluster and shout my way out of potentially scary situations like tree-climbing (broken limbs, callipers for life, wheelchair) or walking the high wall (death, paralysis, crippling injury, plaster casts, or worst of all - being winded).

But, somehow or other, I ended up with Lizzie. Oh, Lizzie, what a potato of a kid you were. She wore round, pink-wire National Health children's glasses and had her fairish hair bowl-cut by her Mother at ear length. Over this coiffure, in all weathers, she wore a beige Fair Isle beret pulled down low all round until it touched her specs. She wore a beige Fair Isle sleeveless, V-neck jumper over her white blouse, a beige Fair Isle cardie and a beige pleated skirt in Crimplene and thick navy blue school knickers with a sweetie pocket. Fawn knee socks, always falling down to her Startrites, completed her inevitable ensemble. She was humourless and stolid, but she was my friend. I have no memory whatsoever of what we talked about, if we did, but I sometimes went to her house which was near the railway line and it fascinated me.

Particularly interesting was the fact she and her nameless younger sisters kept gerbils, not in cages but loose in the front room where they nested in a doll's pram. The girls dressed these bouncy rats in hand knitted baby clothes their Mother made out of fluorescent pink and yellow acrylic wool. The gerbils would streak around the dingy front room like amphetamine nightmare ratbabies, occasionally tripping up over their bonnet strings or a trailing sleeve and hurtling off the sideboard in a death dive. We would rush to their rescue as they lay upside down, their long ratchety hind legs twitching; we'd kiss them better and put them back in the doll's pram where they chittered neurotically before making another mad break for it. Nobody in Lizzie's House of Knitwear seemed to find this odd, but I knew my family would and so I never told them, to keep my Lizzie safe from their scalpel snickering.

Lizzie wasn't allowed officially to be called Lizzie, her Mother used to get very irate about it.

'Can Lizzie come out to play, please?'

'Elizabeth, she's *Elizabeth*, like the Queen, not *Lizzie*, I won't 'ave 'er called Lizzie, d'you hear?'

'Er, yes, Mrs. Umm - can she come out, though, please?'

I'm sure she disapproved as much of me as my family did of poor Lizzie.

Famously, Lizzie got to wear a pink, shiny plastic eye patch, with fluffy white cotton wool underneath because she had a lazy eye - meaning one of her eyes drifted inexorably towards her nose while its muddy hazel companion looked straight at you with Lizzie's usual expression of resignation and faint disbelief. The patch was supposed to train the lazy one to go straight by covering up her one good eye. This meant she could barely see to walk. I was mad with jealousy, as I loved sticky plasters, bandages and all the visible signs of attention and importance. I was addicted to raspberry flavoured children's aspirin, too. Its gritty texture reminded me of my old bead habit. I lay awake at night feverishly coveting the sympathy I felt sure was Lizzie's now she was a 'poor little thing'.

I had a highly coloured vision of illness in other people's homes - my own illnesses, though exciting at the onset, didn't bring me the soft, delicious cuddles, pettings and exquisite invalid food children in books got, and all of which I craved. Rather, I felt very guilty for 'making work', and the concomitant tuts and tooth-suckings thoroughly ruined the joy of illness for me, not to mention, of course, the actual hatefulness of really being sick. But Lizzie's eye patch seemed the perfect solution - no extra work, just the visible wounded soldier effect. It simply wasn't fair. The only time I came near to this Sickie Shangri-La was when I fell down the steps to the park and knocked my front milk teeth out, but apart from the hilarious chorus of 'All I Want For Christmas Is My Two Front Teeth' from all and sundry when I appeared weeping and bloody with my teeth in my hand, the effect I was striving for sadly didn't last longer than a few minutes. I may be quite wrong, but I don't recall ever seeing Lizzie without the eye-patch again. Perhaps she still has it, and if so - well *done*, Lizzie.

I wouldn't want anyone to think I knew no one but Lizzie - it's true that while I didn't have friends, as such, I did play out with the alley boys when I could, and I did know other children, the offspring of my parents friends, that sort of thing. In fact, sometimes there'd be the sort of party where drink was taken dans le jardin; and the partygoers would bring their children, as Nana's small, fully enclosed walled garden was universally admired as the perfect safe playground. However, that proved not to be the case, on one memorable occasion.

It was a brilliant summer's day and the house and garden were full of women in floral prints and pastel shifts, and men in their shirtsleeves and colourful ties. We children were outside on the lawn, playing at some game or other, and being watched over by Nana and a couple of older ladies. Nana's favourite 'Peace' rose was in full bloom, its huge, velvety blossoms of yellow and peach fed by her twin horticultural theories of mulching with used tea leaves and digging in horse manure she collected from the street when the rag-and-bone fella's pony cart went by. The sight of Nana, coal shovel in hand scavenging steaming horseshit from the road before the other gardening grannies could get their scaly claws on it drove Mother to seizures of mortification; but to Nana, standards were one thing, and wasting decent muck was another.

It was the digging in of muck that caused the problem, that bright, garden party day. Nana used an old kitchen knife, its blade worn to a vicious point, the steel dark and grainy, to dig in the little earth bed where the rose grew. I expect she couldn't be bothered to get the correct trowel for such a little garden, and people weren't so accessory obsessed then; the age of the designer gardener wasn't yet upon us. The knife was handy and she used it. She also, for reasons I cannot fathom, often left it stuck in the soil blade up. I'd seen it like that often, and was careful to avoid it; it frightened me just to look at its pared-down iron wickedness.

Now, close to the beautiful 'Peace' rose were the short row of doors leading to the outside toilet, the coalshed and the garage; in fact they were so close, their doors swung out over the flowerbed and Nana was always concerned the roses would be damaged by this, so we were careful. This was a family habit, but of course, the children playing in the garden that day weren't family and no one bothered to instruct them in our ways, as they grew more and more hysterical in the heat and the excitement of playing.

One child was running up and down the path whooping shrilly; suddenly, he leapt onto the slightly open toilet door by the doorknob and started swinging back and forth over the roses, knocking the petals off and screaming. Nana started up and moved towards him to stop him damaging the flowers - I watched in a smug way, waiting for him to be ticked off. Then, in awful slow motion, just as I registered what was underneath his flightpath, he fell off, and onto the old kitchen knife. It stuck straight through the fat part of his outer thigh; I could see the bloody point protruding through his mottled flesh, and the way the lips of the exit wound turned slightly back from the blade. There was a deadly hush, then he began howling like a dog and all hell was let loose. I was fascinated, with the detached unempathic enjoyment of a child witnessing something interesting, if brutal. I cannot imagine how Nana felt. For years I thought she must have been racked with guilt and horror, because that would be what was expected. But if I look back, her face showed no particular expression, even when the child's Mother, scarlet with fear and rage, flecked her face with spittle while accusing her - quite rightly, I fear - of criminal negligence and crass stupidity. Nana just stood, locked into herself, apparently unmoved, her white face, her little ivory monkey's face, still. The whole incident was never spoken of again, to my knowledge, but it accounted for the fact I never had many child targets for the trusty spud gun or the sucker arrows in that apparently perfect little children's garden.

Joolz Denby
(www.joolz.net)

Part Two will be published in Dream Catcher 15

The Fifth Day of Creation

SILENT RAPTURE

I look at her beautiful face and
see the anger

I gaze into her eyes and sense
the hidden tears

I notice her mouth and
taste the bitterness

I carefully observe my fiancee and realize how difficult
this last year has been

My constant travels back home
because of family and business to
a small Caribbean Island she does not really know
But which is so much a part of me

Ooh, God, where have those years gone
We had just graduated from the University
When we could talk, laugh, and
cry about everything and then again
about nothing in particular

Ooh, God, where have all of those years gone
when we could joyfully dance to our own special mixture of classical
Northern rock and roll and sweet
Southern reggae and calypso
Sing loud falsely the moody blues and
make love again and again for entire nights on end in silent rapture
In silent, trembling rapture.

Gregory Gilbert Gumbs

Fenland Bride: A Sequence

(i) Against the Gold

I picture your heart as a map of the Fens:
neat compartments circumscribed
by straitened rivers, artificial cuts;

I haunt the fringes only. Sometimes
I drive and drive just to escape.
The roads are flanked by dykes

so deep an injured biker
lay out of view for days. Here
there is no room for manoeuvre.

As I head for Crowland, the fields
gang up on me, uniform as graph paper;
even the flash of a tulip field neat

as soldiers on parade. I yearn for
the randomness of poppies shaking
their heads blood-wild against the gold.

(ii) Behind the Wheel

Often – on my trips to anywhere – I'd be
slowed by tractors, their huge wheels

spinning out mile after arduous mile
as their exaggerated treads

spewed out a detritus of straw,
a dead confetti floating on the wake

of diesel fumes. I was always the one -
leading a train of frustrated motorists –

who was scared to pull out – even
when the road ahead was clear.

(iii) Catch

Killing time in the museum I read
that eels were used as currency: fifteen hundred
paid a Pinchbeck farmer's rent; four thousand
exchanged hands for building stone from Barnack.

And eels, with waterwolves, pickerels, turbot,
lamprey, perch - were taken, live, to London
in enormous butts. At every stopping place
they changed the writhing water.

In one case is a gleve - a cruel five tined trident
used to spear eels and flip them into boats.
I imagine so much quicksilver stilled
and fading in a watery Fenland dawn.

Next there's an eel hive – a Christmas cracker shape
of wickerwork. I fix my gaze on the empty trap
and when, behind my back, the sun shifts,
a pair of glassy eyes stare back as captured light.

(iv) Tulip Parade

Red tulips signify a love which burns
after the decapitations heads by the million
with hearts so black to show how passion chars:
are pinned to floats in decorative ways
Ferhad a Persian youth adored a maid
paraded to the cheers of day-trippers
called Shirin. When she shunned him Ferhad fled
coachloads clogging the arteries
into the desert, fallow as his hopes;
of this small town. Tamed blooms
his tears sprang to life as tulipan
they will never throw off
named after turbans Turks wind round their heads.
their pursed-lip primness
They slowly stretch exposing all their pain
to let their petals yawn
contorting into acrobatic shapes
in poses of wanton abandon
return to bulbs from which they'll rise again

(v) Gull

Out of the corner of my eye
a gull spells freedom
in this sky of skies. Tricked
into acrobatics by vastness
it loops and gyres without
the safety net of the sea.

Used to the stately glide of ships
it fails to gauge the speed
of the white van. Falls jagged
from the air. I feel the day
contract. No telltale flecks
of a young bird on its feathers –
it was old enough to know better.

Now it lies on the tarmac.
The nearest waves are the brown,
static furrows of a ploughed field:
a place where crows rule.

(vi) HORSESHOE ROAD

I've never had a sense of direction
to lose. Unless the sea's there

I can't say for certain which way
I'm facing. And even if I could

how would I know when a road
is upside down? This one must be –

all the luck's run out, even though
there's no tilt, no hint of a hill.

And when, in need of the drama
of cliffs, I drive to the coast,

the land sinks, abject, to the sea.
I head back across the Fens.

The sea has sucked the heart out.

(vii) SAMPHIRE

Something thrives in this place:
its fleshy leaves – succulent, smooth
and moist with sea spray -
swell from the marsh
A delicacy, I'm told.

Don't pull it up
before the longest day.
Go for those plants
that are washed by every tide.
Fresh water sucks the sap out.

I watch the sea recede. The moon
is late again. Night after night
I soak in a hot bath
praying for blood.

(viii) SOUR MILK

I am not one for reading tea-leaves
but an owl ghosts across the surface
of my coffee on a day when you are out
again. No one has done the shopping.

By daylight the heart that is her face
will fade as ashes in a dying fire.
But at night, over the fens, on silent wings
she will rise, pale as ivory, from the ruins

she makes her home, the buff of her back
dusted with cinder grey. I crush the note
that you have left between indignant fists
and push away the cup. I do not have to drink.

Kathryn Daszkiewicz

FOREFATHER, 1889

Whether or not St Brendan, Erickson or Columbus
discovered America, Caitlin, is irrelevant.
That I, Swinn O'Gallchobhair, single-handedly,
traversed the 2000-mile stretch in a curragh to Boston
with only your face to steer me, to ask your father,
in Irish, for your hand, is surely evidence of love.

Having been blessed with the patience of St Brendan,
I will lie in the byre, watching the grass grow,
counting full moons and apple falls, if need be,
until I hear your father, Caitlin, utter in that soft
Cloughaneeley tongue, the only answer.

Owen Gallagher

THE KISS

On the towpath
couples walk hand in hand
while I hurry past.

A man alone is dangerous,
out of step with himself and the World -
so I've learnt to hurry on,
seek those far away places
where no one else has gone.

I sit on the bridge,
think up all those reasons for a kiss -
love, the betrayal in the Garden,
the touch of lips on a cold face
suppressing the last goodbye.

A barge slips out of the night -
kettles, roses and children blowing kisses
that fly by like arrows into the dark.

Idris Caffrey

A Mirror In Carbridge

Based on Richard Diebenkorn's 1955 painting Berkeley No. 52'

beauty lifted like a vapour
from the untroubled field

I was ready with a breath
behind hotel window glass
my warm body waiting

I was ready with words
a harpoon and an ice axe
to shatter air conditioning

between the blind hill fog
between the dead star mist
beauty rearranged atoms
to encroach on sleep

only glass between us

beauty with its truth
meeting itself and dying
in needy water droplets

my mind was a mirror
all I could do was stare

beauty could not enter

Robin Lindsay Wilson

Small Women Get Closer

Inspired by the work of Alberto Giacometti

I wanted you small
when I did not know
how close you were
and you had no lips

you stood shouting
your measurements
never ever change
it's just a bad picture
in a cheap magazine

but it was impossible
to back track into focus
when you looked
into my eyes

it is always time
for me to look away
and create you independently

it's time to go to work
time to look between
the aspiration
and the daily chore

when you have paid
for all that bad luck
you can come home

I will remember you
naked in cotton clothes

blurred in blurred eyes
just as you really are

Robin Lindsay Wilson

Duchamp's Infra Thin Bridegrooms

between the object and its function
there's the manufactured distance
and the possibility of repetition
when the artist has walked away

even tarnished junkyard faucets
which stop grinning and gushing
when no pretty girls are listening
are wrenched on again -
it is the impulse to create

keep your hands to yourself
passing through the readymades
do not conform to your own tastes

ghost ideas walk unnoticed
through the pristine adult world
in a moment of consciousness
when restraint becomes art

like particles of charm
strangeness and quarks

the coming art is infra thin
and allows you to autograph
on the other side of the paper

if you do not use it on weekdays
and you start pretending to dream

Robin Lindsay Wilson

Snake in the House

Grandpa was at home all day, except when he went to the library or the seniors' centre, so when he reported that a snake was loose in the house, no one doubted his word. He broke the news during dessert at dinner-time.

Mum, who had been out to the magazine office delivering a book report, dropped her fork with a clang.

'A snake? Cool!' Young Arnie grinned widely. 'Was it green?'

Grandpa shook his head. 'Black.'

'How did it get in?' Dad demanded.

It had come Special Delivery in a cardboard box. The courier had thrust a clipboard into Grandpa's face and ordered him to 'Sign here'. Grandpa, who had been roused from a nap and hadn't had his glasses on, scrawled his signature on the dotted line. The delivery man then shoved the box in his hands and departed. Grandpa had assumed that it was a parcel from a publisher containing books for Mum to review. Only after closing the door did he realize that there were air holes. He wrested the box open and out shot a snake, which slithered to the floor and in a flash, had disappeared down the hall. He'd put the box out with the garbage, which had been collected that morning.

'Was it a garter snake or something bigger?' asked Clea, who was fourteen.

'Bigger, and dark,' said Grandpa. 'Like a fan belt, only not circular, of course.'

Mum's face was pale. 'Bob, you're going to have to find it.' She said to Dad. 'If you can't, we'll have to call an exterminator.'

'It's bound to come out sooner or later,' Grandpa said, finishing his caramel pudding. 'It has to eat.'

'To eat!' Droplets broke out on Mum's forehead. Her stomach churned. She was about to dash to the downstairs bathroom, but the thought occurred to her that the snake might be curled around the base of the toilet.

'Barb, relax,' said Dad. 'It's probably on a window sill, looking for flies.' Mum made a gagging sound and fled.

'If I find it, can I take it to school?' Arnie demanded.

'No, you'll release it outside where it belongs,' his father said. Then a smile twitched at his lips. 'It will probably go up to the attic.'

Clea never blinked. Against her parents' wishes, she had moved from her frilly white bedroom to the attic, where she sat on a mattress beneath a sloping ceiling writing her journal as flies buzzed in the warmth of May. The attic was hot in summer and cool in winter, but she didn't mind. She dressed in black, with her hair in a wild array of curls, and didn't care that the preppies called her 'Morticia.' After high school, she intended to move into a loft in New York or a garret in Paris to become an author, not just a book reviewer and feature writer like Mum. If only the snake would creep up to her aerie! She would train it to curl around her arm like a bracelet.

'Was it United Parcel, or Can Par?' asked Dad. Grandpa said he didn't remember.

'That creature obviously had a destination,' Dad said. 'Someone will be missing it. I'll phone the courier services, and Arnie, you get a flashlight and look everywhere that a snake might go.'

'Cool!' Arnie slid off his chair and got the flashlight from the kitchen. There, he shone it under the fridge and the stove. 'There's nothing moving', he reported. Mum, looking greenish but calmer, began clearing the table. Grandpa loaded the dishwasher.

None of the courier services knew anything about a snake. The whole matter was a mystery. Dad wanted to question Grandpa further, but the old man had gone to his ground floor bedroom for the night. Lately he'd been tense and cranky. It was kindest to leave him alone.

Mum telephoned Mavis, the cleaner who came every Thursday. Mavis was reassuring. During her many years of housecleaning, she had dealt with several snakes, and wasn't afraid of them. She also had captured angry wasps buzzing against the window glass, runaway toddlers careering into traffic, and once a feral cat cornered in a basement window well. The only thing was, she would need extra time if she was to search for snakes and do the housework too. Could she extend her hours, say from 1:00 til 5:30 instead of the usual 12:30 til 4:00?

Mum said 'Fine'. The children could go after school to the library or to friends' homes. As a freelance writer for a local magazine, she could find a corner of the office to work in, just this once. Dad was away all day anyway. Grandpa could go to exercise class at the seniors' centre and could stay on for Bridge or Sing-a-long.

That night, Mum and Dad lay in bed talking about the situation. Dad had checked the bedroom baseboards and had looked under the dressers. Only then would Mum retire for the night.

Dad told her that the critter had probably gone to the basement and would get out through one of the air holes in the old-fashioned storm windows that had been on the house ever since Grandpa and Grandma had first bought it. The snake might also exit the house via knot-holes in the attic, slithering to freedom down the eavestrough and drainpipe. Or, it might escape through the kitchen doggie door, unused since Phideaux had passed on. These hypotheses made Mum feel better, and she drifted off to sleep. Dad did too.

In dreams, Mum returned to high school biology class. Tim Parker had been her lab partner. He had held snakes by the head so that they couldn't twist around and strike, though they darted their forked tongues vigorously. With the snake wrapped around his arm like one of those exotic Indian mirrors, she had touched its skin and found it smooth and dry. She admired Tim's confidence, and felt safe with his handling of the snake. She even began to find its darting motions exciting.

She woke at dawn, feeling cross. This snake in the house was just one more little wriggle of fate. Bob was a good man and they had a happy family, but she'd never imagined that at this stage they would be living still, with his father, that she would be writing such fluff, and that her daily life would be a series of minor crises not of her own making. It was unusual for her to be able to catch an uninterrupted hour at her desk in the former maid's room off the kitchen. There she wrote about perennials that thrived in the shade, the challenge of potty learning, and, of course, her books column. Sometimes she thought of that novel that she had begun when she was expecting Clea. These days, novels were formulaic, with mandatory sex scenes, suspenseful sections and car chases at specified intervals. Life wasn't like that. It was more like the situation with the snake. She might be watering the geraniums in her study window some day and find it coiled, its head thrashing, its tongue darting.

She curled up against Dad, who sighed blissfully. He was dreaming of a Boy Scout camping trip. While walking in the long grass, he suddenly felt something creep over his canvas shoe — thrilling yet disturbing. Then his dream fast-forwarded him into the tent at night. Twigs under the mattress nudged his back. His toe, cushioned by his sleeping bag, touched the tent pole. 'Snake,' he thought, without fear, and slept on.

Upstairs, Clea dreamed of Italy, which she had never seen, of wearing pyjamas in the heat, getting water from the well, like D. H. Lawrence in his poem, 'Snake'. As in the poem, the snake appeared, but Clea didn't 'miss [her] chance with one of the lords of life.' She didn't hurl stones at the snake, but sat quietly and watched it drink.

The next morning, while sitting on the toilet, Arnie let out a shriek that brought his parents running. 'I saw the snake!' he shouted. But it was only the cord of his mother's hair dryer, uncurling, pushing out from the cupboard door as if it had a life of its own.

'If we had a dog,' Arnie told her, 'it would have found the snake by now.'

Dad told Arnie to hurry up and get dressed, and went back to the master bedroom. He always wore a suit to work. Reaching into his closet to get a belt, he was startled when something cool and slippery eluded his grasp. Three or four belts fell together. As he picked them up he noted their texture. None of them produced quite the sensation that he'd felt moments before.

Later that day, Mum went to get the small hand vacuum cleaner out of a cupboard to clean up the ashes that Grandpa had left on the rug. Something moved with a zipping sound. She screamed. Grandpa, who had been halfway out of the door on the way to the seniors' centre, came as fast as he could. Together they realized that the cord must have been caught in the door, and had retracted when Mum opened it.

'Thank goodness Mavis comes tomorrow,' Mum said. Grandpa left the house, whistling a cheerful tune.

That evening, as the family gathered in front of the TV, Dad said that he was ready to reopen the dog question, and Arnie cheered. Only Grandpa objected, saying that he was too old to contend with a puppy all day. Arnie stuck out his lower lip. Mum suggested a mature dog from the Humane Society, perhaps a spayed female. Both grandfather and grandson brightened.

Clea was not in on the discussion. She was in her garret drawing a comic strip about a jungle dwelling maiden who wore snakes around her limbs. Boa constrictors did not harm her, because she charmed them. Pythons were her special friends. She planned to offer her comic to Kyle, a boy at school who was starting an underground newspaper.

The following day at 1:00, Grandpa was at home alone, paddling around in his sock feet. He had said that he would be there to let Mavis in. After all, he was responsible for the situation. He watched at the front window for her Volkswagen Beetle to pull into the drive, and when she did, he was at the door to meet her.

Mavis was a sturdy woman with wash-and-wear hair that framed her face like the petals of a daisy. She wore stirrup pants and a T-shirt, and carried nothing in the way of snake traps or nets.

'Are they all gone for the day?' she asked Grandpa, as he closed the door behind her.

'Yes!' He opened his arms wide and she stepped into his embrace.

'You're a wily fellow,' she said. 'What a clever ploy!'

'We never get any time together any more,' he said, but his sentence broke off as Mavis pressed her lips against his.

'They parted for air, 'My son starts his new job at the end of the month,' she said. 'He'll be out of my place by then.'

'Good!' said Grandpa.

'So, how's the snake?' she asked him.

Grandpa chuckled. 'Quiet at the moment, but I'm sure when you find him you'll stir him up.'

'I'll do my best,' she said, smiling. 'I expect it will be hard. Maybe I should start in your bedroom.'

That day when Mum returned, the house smelled of lemon polish and freshly brewed coffee. Grandpa, looking relaxed from his afternoon at the seniors' centre, was having a coffee with Mavis at the kitchen table. All aglow from her strenuous day, Mavis apologized for failing to find the snake. She had, however, seen some markings on the living room carpet which suggested that it had slithered over to the window and out through a hole in the screen.

'Oh, I hope so!' Mum poured herself a cup of coffee and sat with them at the table. Her blue pant suit matched her eyes, and Grandpa complimented her on her appearance.

'How was your day?' he asked.

'I enjoyed the office,' she said. 'My editor said that I may work there anytime I want. It actually gave me a lift.'

'That's important,' Grandpa said gravely. Mavis nodded wisely.

Ruth Anne Latta

Sonar

Sleep, like water, seeped into the rooms,
rose some way up the walls
and drenched my books, the lamp, the sheets.

Our bodies slowed beneath the weight,
stilled to just the odd, absentminded heartbeat.

My flung arm shifted from his shoulder, came adrift,
a current dragged my ponderous mass away.

The salt-flood buoyed me, warmed me. I heard
the heave of his chest, like shingle, then,

the thud of a beat, and my reply:
a pip in the either, each time duller, the silence

more protracted as I drifted underneath the kitchen table,
on, towards the open water of the building's stairwell.

Kate Potts

Currawong

The things that ignore us in the end save us - Andrew Harvey

He won't come closer
though I spoon out mango
flesh and flick it

within a yard of his tangled refuge.
Weightless, like a spaceman, he hangs,
an immaculate sun for an eye,

wheeling somewhere our thing-
heavy minds can't fathom.
He won't sing either.

He keeps his peace,
knowing the world
turns on it.

We wash plates and cups, shake
crumbs to the baked earth,
file to the car.

I feel triumph
that he gave no ground,
that his pristine labyrinth

can't be cracked by hungry algorithms.
The seat burns my fingertips.
I glance back.

He straddles a shimmering heap,
black
beak reared skyward,

letting the wise juice caress his throat.
Then we're a shrinking drone beyond the eucalyptus.
Something is saved.

It's dawn again
in the world.
The song can begin.

Sydney, 2nd November 2001

Stephen Parr

Slow Burn

Left out and yellowing by the lounger,
Culture from the weekend broadsheet:

the bearded middle aged columnist,
all chest, pocketed hands and brogues

stares out from his by-line,
finding more and more of life

less and less to his liking;
his words and gaze folded outwards

to slow burn, discolouring
with fertile spores of misanthropy.

At sundown the process is arrested -
- words flap in the breeze

like the wasp, frantic for sweetness
at the bottom of the glass.

Adrian Buckner

RESORT

I have sensed the awesome grip
of the river's wrestling currents
and watched the sharp light
scrape it's surface silver
and I've heard the gull's coarse calling
as they battle on scraps of plenty;
and the happy slap and splash
of hidden seals.

I have seen the litter of lust
that is forgotten in the morning
heard children cry and tears drip
from a granite woman's cheek.

And I've heard the booming
boasts of men
that echo

along the front

across the beach

down the years

and I've wondered at my place in all of this.

Gordon Wilson

Days out at Scarborough

The Grecian temple opens to a seagull sky.
The organist plays pensioners' requests.
Summer after summer his portly fingers
stun the keys to a willing submission.
Roses of Picardy perfume the rain-soaked
promenade, on a bad day under the umbrellas.
Feet tap to a selection from *Carousel.*

Today, the pillars and fancy pediments
of pure white plasterboard
rock to *Rule Britannia* and sea shanties.
The keep-fit fanatic, hides his bus pass,
his brown well-oiled body naked
from the waist up, sings from his deck chair.
Refusing to be a slave, he waves
a Union Jack with great gusto.
Saucy blonde widows and
born-again singles give him the eye.
His neighbour, handkerchief tied
to bald pate for protection, joins in
clapping his hand to keep the beat.
His wife opens the sandwich box.

On the sand the donkeys wait for customers,
their gentle pace too slow.
Reared on computers, the children play the arcades,
putting money in fruit machines.
All-day breakfasts and fish & chips
do a good trade.
Mussels cockles and shrimps wilt delicately
in their saucers of vinegar.
All around the bay, pleasure boats shout
at one another through loud-speakers.
At the top of the cliff, nursing a deaf ear,
the castle crumbles.

Amyon Corbould

The Silence

I've carried it inside me all my life,
somewhere between abdomen and epiglottis.
It follows its own seasons, swells like ripe fruit
plugging the larynx, or shrinks to a stone hard pit.

When I was younger they thought me possessed,
taken over by some cuckoo spirit.
They'd talk in loud measured words as if I were simple.
It flourished in the blank stares I chose to answer with.

When I speak now it shivers like a conscience,
troubled at what I might not mean to say, intervenes
by cutting me off mid-sentence, plays cat and mouse
with words, scrambles syntax. I go unheard in meetings.

It shuns town centres, supermarkets, heavy traffic,
muzak in the yoga class; flings a curse of deafness
at Tornado pilots savaging the air,
stalls chainsaws in a vice of elm.

From time to time it blossoms, insists on space.
That's when I'll lock the door, unplug the phone.
Printed words become a chanting mob
so all the books get shelved, newspapers binned.

Bass winds might tune up in the chimney
or rain make idle talk against the windows.
I sit, count breaths. The stove ticks. The alembic
of the gut ferments, the blood's hydraulics roar.

Eventually, in full flower,
it'll have me to itself. I'll listen out
for currents in the air, my thoughts
retreating voices in a garden.

Mike Barlow

The Station Master

From the diary of a stationmaster on the Kalda Railway
somewhere in central Russia

1. It's February something. Started work today
as stationmaster on the Kalda line.
The station's just a wooden shack
with a mud floor, a bed, a desk,
an ancient stove — all mine.
Oh, and a telegraph...

I think of thousands of slender telegraph poles
looping their way across the steppes,
like a rescue rope I may some day be glad of...

I've never felt so quite marooned,
and yet, for reasons which I can't disclose,
I need to live alone.

Alone I am. A human full stop
at the end of this Kalda railway line
which crawling towards its target Kalda, died
some fifty miles away on the frozen steppe.
Poor management. The cash refused to flow.
They couldn't even pay the men to lay
the last few rails, now buried in the snow.

2. February 10th. A passenger told me so.
An hour before dawn the morning train steamed in.
The passenger, the only one, knocked at my door.
Still in the greatcoat I sleep in, shabby and worn,
I let him in and watched his squat on the floor.
I got back to bed, then begged him to make the tea
(I detailed how) and we had a nice drink and a chat.
Company I find means quite a lot to me.

3. Still bitterly cold today.
No passengers.
Three natives shuffled across the fields
to sound me out. Brought bearskins, sacks of potatoes
to trade. They expected to haggle. I accepted their price.
They stayed an hour or so to talk, then left,
shaking their heads as they went,
boots crunching the ice.

4. You'd think the top soil would thaw a bit in March.
But no. All day dug freezing holes for seeds.
Like breaking stones. I've started much too soon.
These seeds and tubers will never show.
A cold weighs on my chest.
Must turn in now.

5. Yesterday was weird. An inspector came
to check my books and take my ticket cash.
A podgy man, he wore a suspicious stare
as if he thought I was the sort to stash
the company's roubles away behind the stove.
Without a word, he opened my ledger and stabbed
a random entry with a prosecuting finger.
'Accounting error!' he growled, 'whole column invalid!'
I had to guide him down the income page
to demonstrate that all my figures tallied.
And then he changed his tack: 'You haven't sold
a bunch of tickets, have you? Can't go on
much longer like this. We'll have to close the line.'
'Well that would put pay to two jobs, yours and mine.'
He cheered up when I brought out schnapps and glasses
and started singing sentimental songs,
and then we talked and in the end, as one
hurled insults at the feckless Railway Board
and bellowed endless verses of 'Kalinka'
and utterly pissed collapsed together on

the bed in a tight embrace and slept like that
for ten whole hours...

This morning I stood to attention by the train
to salute my superior as he climbed into
an empty carriage where he gently fell
asleep again.

6. I sometimes dream about that phantom town
the railway never reached, but as for news
I see the Kalda Star from time to time.
Saw one today a boarding traveller dropped.
'Keep it,' he said, 'it may amuse.'
Scandal abounds in Kalda, corruption, vice
but stories lack beginnings, middles, ends.
I still don't know why the magistrate hanged himself
or who were the mayor's suspected lady-friends.
I was pleased to read that Ivan the Wielder of Axes,
a serial hero, chopped off his rival's head
and led his beautiful bride to church
and then they went to bed.

That made my day.

7. I've been misled most grievously.
They said the woods were stinking hot with game.
I even paid a deposit on a gun.
But since I've been here
I haven't clapped eyes on
a single deer.

But we do have rats.
When they hear the engine's distant whistle
they swarm across the fields like refugees
desperate to catch the last train to the border.
They're trying to wreck my station by degrees.

I hear them scrabbling as I try to sleep.
They burn hot holes through wood like drill-bits.
I light a candle to catch the moment when
their teeth and claws break through...

8. My first three months are up. The snow has turned
slush. The buds on that single silver birch
are easing open in the April sun.

I'm down with whooping cough, a kid's complaint.
Day in, day out I howl like a wolf in a trap.
I greet the a.m. train with a fanfare of howls.
Doubled up on my bench I whoop into my lap.
I take the herbal tea the train driver swears by,
so far to no effect.
My hand shakes as I write.
Beads of sweat gather and drop on my forms
where I note nil-returns.
I need to see a doctor.
There are doctors...
There are said to be doctors in Kalda...

10. A few spring days in Kalda
will see me through...

11. Must telegraph for a relief.
A relief stationmaster?
My God, what a job!

Based on the story *Erinnerung an die Kaldabahn*
in one of Franz Kafka's diaries

David Gill

Prisoners

Their affectionate uncle
escaped from prison
and went to prison in England.

He took his torturer with him.

Free over there, he could live,
he could write his articles;
all he had learnt by heart
he could pour into unrhymed lines,
into open-ended stanzas.

If he didn't write,
then his nieces, both newly married,
could lie awake in the early hours
unworried about their doors,
how their quietly altered addresses,
almost unseasoned timber,
at the first kick
would splinter in on them,

and he would still be in prison.

Hubert Moore

ID

required for those visiting asylum-seekers held in detention

A passport will do. Otherwise
all they need is a modest
collection of poems, title and name
on the front, and a face-only
photo of the author himself
looking poetic on the back.

You get through the gate and they frisk you,
strip each poem from the page
and make it stand with its arms out.
They finger the ribbed cage of the lines,
count syllables, check for a rhyme-scheme
strapped to the calf or thigh.

OK, they sigh in the end. Yet again
they've found nothing, certainly not
anger, the small explosive
you flatter yourself you concealed
at time of writing - to go
decorously off in the white

silences between stanzas.

Hubert Moore

A Refugee Concept

(i)
I have always thought
that rivers are cursed
for they have no place
to go but into the sea

No home once you start
to run and Stumble blindly
over the stones Wind around
things you cannot go through

The swelling force is not life
giving but Your desperate desire
that speeding up the way down
will make you empty yourself out

(ii)
Whether they are re-routed or Dammed
Made to burst their banks
their fate is in someone else's hands

When completely dried out
They still harbour that unreal hope
their beds are proof enough they existed

They are the measure of suffering
that cannot be measured They are
eternal rejects of God's mercifulness

(iii)
I am one of them, Whose past,
running behind me, and with me,
and ahead of me, is the only present,

Whose words are drops that drown
in themselves, Whose viscous silence
at the estuary is the abandoned presence.

Mario Susko

Snow Blind

We woke to winter's white machinery
cogged on the window pane,
kicked open the sash with the hand's heel
and drew a cold into our heads
sharp as the shock of peppercorn.
You dressed for four seasons
and I, stoked on a stove's hot breakfast,
put two layers to the test - regretted it.

Before I'd found my gloves you remarked
on the blood of last autumn's moon
trapped beneath my fingernails. In turn
I noted each small madness as you took
to the bedded down lane:
eyes moth white in the snowfall,
arms propellored outwards -
every move a fidget of light,
every dance a sycamore key,
every turn a wrong one.

John Lindley

Our Son

Quarter to three: I wake again at the hour of his birth.
Thirty years ago and now he paces corridors of dark
In nightmares of self-condemnation where random thoughts
Besiege his fevered imagination — England's
Imminent destruction, his own, the world's...

Sixty to eighty cigarettes a day, unavailing depot injections,
Failed abscondings, failed everything: Eton to Balliol
Hold no sway on ward one, nor even being
'A six language master,' on PICU madness is the only qualification.
There was the 'shaving incident' at school, which
Made him ready to walk out at fifteen, the alcohol
Defences at Oxford which shut us out then petered out
During the six years in India, studying Bengali at Shantiniketan.

He tottered from the plane, penniless and unshaven,
To hide away in the seediest bedsit Beeston could boast
Where night turned to day and vaguely he applied
For jobs as clerk and court usher and drank in pubs with yobs.

When the crisis came — 'I feel my head coming off my body' —
I was ready and unready, making the necessary calls
To get a bed, to keep him on the ward, to visit and reassure
Us both that some way out could be found.

The 'Care Home' was the next disaster, trying to cure
Schizophrenia with sticking plaster: 'We don't want
Carers' input, we call patients 'residents' and insist on chores
Not medication', then the letters of terrible abuse, the finding of a flat,
'The discharge into the community.'
His 'keyworker' was the keyworker from hell: the more
Isaiah's care fell apart the more she encouraged
Him to blame us and 'Make his life his own', vital signs
Of decline ignored or consigned to files, 'confidentiality' reigned supreme.

Insidiously the way back to the ward unveiled
Over painful months, the self-neglect, the inappropriate remarks
In pubs, the neglected perforated eardrum, keeping
Company with his feckless cousins between their bouts in prison.

The pointless team meetings he was patted through,
My abrupt dismissal as carer at the keyworker's instigation,
The admission we knew nothing of, the abscondings we were told of
And had to sort out, then the phone call from the ASW.
'We are about to section your son for six months, have you
Any comment?' Then the final absconding to London
From a fifteen minute break on PICU, to face his brother's
Drunken abuse, the police were kindness itself as they drove him
to the secure unit.

Two nurses came by taxi from Leeds the next day to collect him.
The Newsam Centre's like a hotel — informality and first class treatment.
Behind the locked doors he freezes before and whispers
'Daddy, I was damned in hell but now I am God's friend.'

Note: PICU: Psychiatric Intensive Care Unit;
ASW, Approved Social Worker

Barry Tebb

Their Little Secret

Anne had been feeling bad all day. Once she was home from the office she rushed upstairs to the toilet, dropping her sanitary pad on the lino before sitting down. What was wrong with her bladder? She hadn't been boozing lately - she and John had decided to have one last try at starting a family. Glancing at the brown pad she sighed - another month wasted. They'd already wondered about IVF. Neither of them dared to admit they were that desperate and besides, the doctor had said that there was no biological problem. But they had the money. Perhaps now was the time. Picking the pad up she saw something moving, like a caterpillar, but thinner, hairier. Don't panic, she thought, it probably just crawled there. She carried the pad to the kitchen, dropped it in an empty jam jar, screwed the lid on loosely and put it on the shelf.

The deep freeze was full of sauce for lasagne; they made litres at a time. She defrosted it, slapped on layer after layer and put the tray in the oven, and then to get away from the heat she sat on the patio reading the free newspaper. It was one of her favourite places - she could smell the herbs they'd planted, their scents mingling in the April sun. A sprig made all the difference to a ready-made meal. Vegetables covered the far end of their otherwise tidy garden. Friends joked about their knobbly carrots. Sometimes they entered the ugly vegetable section of local horticultural shows, though they never won.

When she heard the front door slam she picked some oregano and went inside. 'You look flushed', John said, holding her.

'John, there's something I want to show you'. She gave him the jam jar. 'Have you ever seen anything like this before?'
He held it to his face, rotated it. 'I'd say it was a sanitary towel. Wings?'

'Look more closely'

' I can see a false eyelash. Oh', he said with a start, 'It's moving. I'd take it to the doctor it I were you. Could be a tape-worm'.

She left it in the kitchen that night, taking a photo before she went to bed. They didn't mention it again until John returned home the next day.

'So, did you take your little pet to the doctors?' he asked.

'No. Look.'

She held up the jar. The creature had grown wider, a buff of membrane with hair along one edge.

They both had tough jobs. Entertaining clients and drinking with workmates on Friday made up their social life. They'd begun to welcome quiet evenings at home. In the weekends they would go walking. It was hard to keep up visits to friends when they all had kids. In bed when they'd both put their books aside and turned their bedside lights off, he started stroking her stomach.

'So what do we do?' she said turning away, 'About the jam jar'

'Tomorrow we go to the library and look through the medical books. It's a parasite of some sort'

'Yuck'

'It's common enough. I saw a programme about them recently. There are more parasites on Earth than hosts. Some of them are really clever too. There's this fish parasite which needs to get into birds to reproduce so it makes the fish wriggle about near the surface'

'What do we feed it?'

'I don't know. It seems to be thriving as it is. More blood?'

Next day the rain prevented them from going to the library. Then John had to go away on a business trip for a week. He phoned to tell her how he'd got two bookshop chains interested in a new series of travel books, then realising he'd been talking too much about himself asked 'How's your little friend?'

'It's spreading out. It's grown a sort of cyst under the membrane'

'I don't think it will last long'

'It's healthy though. It'll soon be too big for the jar'

They went to the aquarium section of the local garden centre when he returned, amazed by the aisles of accessories available. They bought a fishtank, and chose a model shipwreck for it. Once home she shook the creature into its new home, adding a lettuce leaf, a saucer of milk, and her latest tampon. In its new surroundings it seldom moved, sliding more slowly than a slug. John hadn't looked at it for a while. It was puce, resembling a lumpy omelette, softly pulsing. A slit went almost from one side to the other. There were 2 cysts now, each with a crescent of hair.

'You know what it is don't you?' said Anne.

'Tell me'

'Our baby'

'Don't be crazy. I've been playing along but now I think it's gone far enough'

'They're not cysts, they're eyeballs, and the eye-lashes are just like yours'

He was shocked for a moment, then she laughed and hugged him.

But it kept growing until they had to remove the shipwreck. Her period never stopped so there was always a supply of food. She added slices of fruit and leftovers. Some disappeared over night, some were left covered in dried slime. She began to spend more time in the kitchen just so she could look at it. Over night it sprouted 2 ribbony tails.

'I think one of us should come home lunchtimes to check it's ok', she said.

'I won't stop you'

'Why should it be me?'

'Because you work closer. Besides, I don't wear tampons'

'Fair enough, but remember you bleed John, you still bleed. How do we look after it though?'

'I don't know. We could phone the zoo I suppose'

'No they'll take it away'

'Ask the doctor. You're going to have to ask about your period anyway. Until it stops we're not going to get anywhere really. You're not getting any younger. It's as much psychological as anything else. Once the pressure's off, things might just happen. That's what they say'

'No, they won't understand. They'll say it's a freak. We can't tell anyone. We're on our own'

We'd better move it out of the kitchen then, in case we have guests.'

'Guests? Who? Who bothers with us nowadays?'

Nevertheless, they carried the tank to their bedroom, putting a sheet over it when they were both out.

He still played badminton most Thursdays, but videos had replaced cinema trips, and they no longer went out with office colleagues. When they talked to each other in company or on the phone from work they referred to it as 'our pumpkin', or pretended to describe the latest growth of their carrots that were nothing like the ones in Waitrose. They cancelled their holiday to Morocco. Anne felt anxious whenever she left the house. She often sat on the bed listening to the radio and reading. She never brought home a parenting magazine, but browsed through them in newsagents. She began to realise how parents lived in a different world to the one she and John inhabited. Her friends with young families were puzzled by her phone calls about nothing in particular.

She took a photo each day after she cleaned the tank, keeping the rolls of film in her underwear drawer. Its tails grew toes. Even John couldn't deny that the bumps and hollows had formed into a face, a sort of a face. Sometimes in the night they could hear soft slurping noises. Its skin was damp. Ears appeared, or so she thought until they extended and grew pointed fingers.

When he came home one day she was crying.

'He wasn't in the tank at lunchtime. I thought he'd been stolen'

'He?'

'Yes. I'll show you later. I looked everywhere. He was under the bed. He must have fallen somehow. But he's ok. Just a little bruise'

'I'll put some books on the lid so it won't come off'

'What shall we tell our parents?'

'Nothing. Not now, not ever. It's a secret we'll have to live with for the rest of our lives for everyone's sake'

'Shouldn't I wear a bump under my blouse? If we suddenly appear pushing a pram no-one will think he's ours'

'I don't think we should make those kinds of plans. 5 months old now isn't it?

'Not it', she said, 'he. Look.'

In the following weeks changes were rapid. Flesh grew to fill the gap between the top of the spindly legs. A neck formed just above the arms to separate the mass into a head and a torso. When the bones grew his movements changed. He no longer rolled and slid. His limbs no longer bent like a rag doll's when she lifted him. He could stretch, and when he did he nearly filled the tank. John began to wonder whether maybe things might work out ok in the end. Sometimes Anne cut a finger and dripped the blood into the tank, just in case he was thirsty.

She found him one morning curled up in a corner of the tank, knees to chin, eyes open and staring at the wall. She screamed for John. He jumped from the bed and reached in, felt him clammy and cold, then put a sheet over the tank.

'It was bound to happen sooner or later'

'Why?' she said 'What did we do wrong?'

'It was a miscarriage. There are probably specimens like this frozen in every hospital. It's not the kind of thing they publicize. We'll try again. We'll get over this. It's not too late'

'We didn't give him enough love. You never once held him. You never believed me', she said, throwing herself on the bed.

'We did all we could', he said, 'It's the only way. We'll try again'

John had already planned what to do. After the neighbours had gone to work, he dug a big hole amongst the spreading pumpkin plants. He brought an empty fertiliser bag in from the shed, he picked up the dead body, gave it to Anne who hugged it then returned it to John. Slipping the body into the bag he cupped the head. He didn't know much about babies but he was sure it was far too light. He studied the face - not so much a child's face as a face drawn by a child. On the way to the garden he fumbled in her drawer for the rolls of film and slid them into the bag before carrying it outside as nonchalantly as possible under his arm.

Tim Love

The Wireless

My father's lone campaign was won:
the first TV we ever had
usurped the long held pride of place
his mother's wireless had enjoyed
until her surrender in '54.

That day, he thought,
must surely mark the future
breaking through.
But something jammed the signal
where we lived,

so all we saw was a snowy screen
as black-and-white blizzards
hit everything —
(five minutes at most
of that was enough

to leave us snow-blind
for another ten!)
Not one to give in easily,
my father was a stubborn man
who took root

in front of his precious set,
down on one knee
for half the night,
struggling to tune both channels in:
which did no more

than make each little snowy dot
grow to twice the size it was:
total whiteout and in the glare
we watched what
meagre ghosts there were

all disappear...
When all else failed,
he'd scramble up onto the roof
and thunder about like an angry Zeus,
brandishing the aerial

like lightning
in his massive hands,
determined to get the picture clear.
But still each episode
saw Tarzan lost

in snowstorms that blasted
his jungle home — Enough
was enough, even for him,
my father threw the towel in — I
lip-read my grandmother's

silent *Amen...* To her
it was anathema,
a curse of graven images
across the screen
when pictures make to tell us

what words mean.
Listening with her
to the wireless again,
I learned to love how words disclose
what does not correspond to anything.

Tony Flynn

Waiting Love

I pretend I am waiting for my boyfriend.
We are all waiting for our boyfriends, they laugh.
Just waiting love. Waiting here.
I can hear the noise my shoes make
and the sound of traffic.
We're all waiting for our boyfriends here -
listen mate, listen to my shoes.
I'm just walking love. Walking here.
I wish I was in a quiet room with a grand piano
waiting for my husband to come and light the candles.
The servant has polished the marble floor
and I can see my heels falling on it.
He'll be here in a minute. Any minute.
We are all waiting for our boyfriends here
we laugh. And look - the seagulls
have come inland - it's a sure sign
of a storm love. Come on, let's go inside
and wait. The candles are lit
and the marble floor is polished like silk.
Breathe on it and your breath will freeze
forever. Waiting here...
The floors are like silk. The candles are lit.
The music
has started.
De we dance now?
I am waiting for my partner.
Who is it
I'm waiting for?
We're all waiting love. Waiting here.

Elizabeth Stott

Letting The Side Down

Through a welter of distractions it had come to Elspeth somehow that in the course of her long bereavement she had either neglected to give presents at all or had given ones which were inappropriate, sometimes grotesquely so. Probably to do with her pills: either she forgot to take them or, to make up for this, she took too many, her behaviour wildly erratic as a result. In some quarters, that's to say, her reputation was for meanness, in others for eccentricity, in others for a kind of crazed generosity.

In a large family there was no escaping it. All those brothers and sisters and nephews and nieces: in the bright surfaces of their affection or suspicion or derision she glimpsed herself, dumb one moment, grinning through loose teeth the next, expostulating the next, a shambling figure largely lost to herself and the world. She saw that there was much ground to make up if her reputation was to be restored, for hadn't her husband said to her, not long before he died, 'Whatever else you do, Elspeth, don't let the side down. Don't let the side down.'

If the injunction still sounded disturbingly in her head, that didn't mean she was entirely sure what it meant. She had perhaps understood at the time, but these days, so confused and distracted was she, so lost, she couldn't be sure she understood anything very well.

One of her fears was that her bereavement might never end and that her husband would take advantage of this to control her from beyond the grave. The possibility unhinged her further. Sometimes she would be moved to fantastic displays of defiance which, like flocks of birds, would fly wildly upwards, but only as far as a ceiling of imprisoning glass – only as far as that. Then she would be desperate again, stumbling from room to room touching things, tapping them, like a blind woman.

In the tenth month of her bereavement she found her diaries again, and this was a help, for she learnt that, unless her reasoning had been affected here also, one of her favourite nieces, Anna, was to be twenty-one in a fortnight's time.

She couldn't bring herself to work out which birthdays and anniversaries she had missed, however: it was too embarrassing. Nor which occasions she had marked with ridiculous presents. Which ridiculous presents? She thought she could remember a gaudy tricycle and a vast inflatable gorilla which toppled over immediately it was inflated and a CD entitled the 'The World's Funniest Jokes' and trousers and dresses and sweaters which for reasons unclear to her hadn't impressed their recipients.

In the hurly-burly of presents in a constantly changing world, though, in which the money in your bank and purse went up and down with the markets, how carefully noted were ridiculous gifts? Did anyone sit in judgement over presents, grading them, from the marvellous to the ridiculous? With so many being given and received, the air thick with them, dark with them, as it sometimes seemed to Elspeth, did anyone care that much?

She hoped to hear from the ancient silence which bred in the rooms about her that no one did, but she heard that, on the contrary, it was a common practice, a very common practice. One which included her own family, too, who should be ashamed of themselves, she thought, somehow challenged to bear witness, not to what was being given, but to how it was being given. The act of giving, she told herself with a kind of broken fervour, surpassed the thing given. People had forgotten that. There could be such a grace in the giving that what was given became almost irrelevant, shrunk to vanishing point.

Sometimes she would find herself smiling as at some approaching consummation. She would clap her hands and make exultant noises, often the noises taking her by surprise, seeming to be not quite hers but to come from some twin or doppelganger in the shadows behind her. Her conviction appeared to be that she need never be confounded by an anniversary again. She would always be able to carry it off memorably: if it wasn't an exemplary entrance, it would be an exemplary smile or handshake or speech. An energy which was at once that of contempt and rage and grief told her so, blowing through her days like a wind (indeed, she often had an astonished, windswept look, her hair awry, her eyes light, faraway).

She thought that if she were to avoid making a fool of herself or actually disgracing herself she should simply do what seemed right. Sometimes her husband would be crouched by the wayside, watching her, indicating approval one moment, disapproval the next. She would talk back at him volubly – her grief permitted it – insisting that often it was not clear how she should behave, that unless she was to hold back and do nothing she should be allowed to act on impulse, generously. She would shout her justifications into the void. Could it be wrong if she didn't feel it was? When she found herself sitting in the garden, for instance, waiting to see if death in any of its many forms was going to appear, a place set for her husband, or for death (she wasn't sure that she would know the difference), was she conducting herself foolishly? Or sitting at the piano trying to recall pieces she had played as a child, singing them to herself in a wavering voice – was this wrong, wanton, a waste of the afternoon? Or refusing to answer the 'phone because she couldn't be bothered to or didn't want to alarm whoever it was by seeming dotty, out of control, deranged – was this wrong? And if all these things were foolish or wrong – by whose standards were they so? 'I mean,' she would cry, 'how can you possibly know!?'

She would regularly remind herself that she was thought inconsistent, with a reputation for meanness in some places, crazy generosity in others. This alone upset her. Otherwise she didn't care how she was regarded, one of the blessings of grief being that, so utterly were you in another world, you didn't care and probably never would again.

At the wrongness or irrelevance of most views of herself, in fact, she would laugh until it hurt, sometimes until she retched. Savage laughter, breaking her up, forcing her into the most peculiar positions: down on one knee, as in supplication; legs apart, head back, howling at the sky; rocking slowly backwards and forwards, a kind of sombre ecstasy; digging her fists into her sides as if sides were the heart of all disturbance; running, bent double, wetting herself.

She had been told that there were magazines which gave advice on presents. What to give and on what sorts of occasions to do so. Carefully graded suggestions for the wealthy. You couldn't go far wrong if you studied such magazines, apparently. So for her niece, Anna's, twenty-first she did briefly study them. Not to let the side down. As through an endlessness of pentecostal distractions she would peer at them, searching for sober ideas. She couldn't read for long, though, without being overcome by boredom or laughter. The roll of a drum to accompany her when she approached Anna: it was the only thought she had.

Had she still been allowed to drive, Elspeth would probably have parked her car in a nearby copse and made her way to Anna's on foot. She took a taxi instead, offering the driver fifty pounds to look after the dog while she made a first, speculative approach to the big house.

For an hour or so people had been arriving to give their presents and offer congratulations. Well before she came close to the house a second time Elspeth could hear, through the still dusk of late September, sounds of unusual merriment. For some reason she imagined a moving staircase with Anna standing on a platform at the top receiving her presents one by one, immediately handing them, for safekeeping, to someone specially hired for the purpose. Not only did the moving staircase seem to have been energised by the occasion, the big house did so too, also the grounds – through which, for days now in her imagination, Elspeth had been walking, her long dress, bought with such gatherings in mind, held a little off the ground.

She wasn't so overwrought she didn't realise that by now just about all the presents would have been given and received, given in a variety of styles, received in just one – Anna's fixed, carefully tutored girlish gratitude. Regardless of the present, that would have been her manner: she wouldn't have deviated from it, she was such a well brought up girl, not one to act as if presents could change your life.

As for the presents, Elspeth's hunch was that they would already be on display. By looking through one of the ground floor windows she'd be able to see them. (She had no illusions about how she would appear, a gleefully curious old hag peering out of the autumn darkness with a high colour and teeth which moved whenever she spoke or smiled or laughed). They would be arranged as in a vast shop window, guests walking round them or standing before them, deep in wonder.

And so it proved. In room after room the furniture had been pushed back not just to accommodate the guests whether standing or dancing but to accommodate and indeed highlight the presents. It had to be imagined that here was everything a young woman could desire. There were skirts and dresses either hanging or draped carefully over the backs of chairs; there was a CD system commanding in its silvery compactness; there was a desk of white wood with, a few feet away, a widescreen television on a stand; there were hats and gloves and scarves on a sideboard, piles of them; bottles of champagne and rows and rows of champagne glasses; enormous bouquets of flowers and more clothes then, hung, Elspeth was sure, so that they could be stroked or fingered in the passing. There was a bicycle and a set of golf clubs and a tennis racquet and a horse's saddle . . .

All these things Elspeth saw or thought she saw, though she couldn't always be sure which were presents and which permanent features of the house. It didn't really matter, she thought, for finally all belonged to the one world, proudly constituting it. Flitting from window to window, her thoughts ran free. She saw other presents in other rooms, gadgets too new for her to name, antiques only half emerged from the shadows but gleaming, glowing, as though polished by experts. And the longer, from quiet darkness peering into bright light, she bore witness to the occasion, the more the presents, like the guests, seemed to be caught up in a gravely endless dance of celebration and renewal. She even fancied that she could hear the music to which all were moving. . .

It astonished her that she hadn't been noticed. It was as if she didn't exist. Once or twice in her eagerness she pressed her face to the windowpane, misting it. There was only glass between herself and the guests, but it seemed an immensity, as if they came from different worlds, as if there was a great silence.

She thought how old her brothers and sisters looked since she had properly seen them last. Some weren't moving at all easily. The children were growing up, however: there was no doubt about that, no one remaining in childhood now. With peculiar intensity she was able to imagine the hopeful young bodies beneath the clothes. The birthday girl herself: in one room for a moment or two she seemed to be virtually naked on a sofa, smiling at her admirers. The well coached smile was barely up to it though. Then she saw a hole in Anna's face where the smile had been and pictured her in her grave. 'Relax!' she cried at once to her niece and herself. 'Relax!'

A few times she came close to tapping on the windowpane to gain Anna's attention. She would be speaking to her later, of course, when she arrived with her present. But by then it might be too late. She might find the house emptied of guests, become a kind of present itself, offered to Elspeth by the night and the silence. She would refuse of course, skipping round the house to make this very clear, skipping round it until she met her husband coming the other way, a bully tonight, if ever there was one, angry in his shroud and desperate to catch her eye.

Let off its lead by the taxi driver, the dog bounded towards her. A hound rather than a dog, she thought, a burly but entirely innocent creature, strong-chested and playful, two years old, it had attracted her attention immediately she entered the cat and dog home a week ago.

Now in the deep autumn night it tried to jump up on her, but she stepped aside, pointing ahead of her. Wherever she pointed it would immediately go. It trotted before her down the drive. She heard it snorting and snuffling in the darkness and, when they came within the arc of light cast by the house, she saw that every few yards it looked back to check that she was still there. Occasionally in sudden glee it would run forwards, growling in mock savagery, a sound, she was content to think, which belonged to the evolutionary past of its kind rather than to this evening on the drive leading to the big house.

Approaching the house, Elspeth felt as if, inspired by the hound, she was taking enormous strides. It came when she called, sprinted away when she threw up an arm, but, whatever it did, she seemed to be doing it, too. It had no name, it was true, but Anna could find one for it, couldn't she, the last of her presents and, almost certainly, the only one in need of a name.

If she were to offer the dog as a present at this late hour, entering the house with it triumphantly, it might be hard for the guests to conceive of them apart. They would be seen as an item, denounced or celebrated as such. It would be as if she were venturing a sort of compound gift, the hound and herself, herself and the hound. If so, so be it. So be it.

It was with a kind of joyous intemperance that the hound, followed closely and excitedly by its mistress, bounded towards the front door which, as though in the hands of some watchful butler, began slowly to open.

Peter Gilmour

Beyond the Branches of that Oak

I Have Fallen In Love With The Forth Bridge

Strapping girders,
lusty arches:
the span of my ambition,
shore to shore
you link me with the old bones,
the new ways,
the true trains that take me
down the path of all my loves.
You lift up your wide arms
to take in the tide,
roll with the shaking wind
that whistles in the rushes
of the wild banks.
You thrill me with your size,
your strong embrace;
you roar with achievement,
you make me proud:
I could hug you.
Let me take the Queensferry train,
slide through you to freedom.
The pipes play
and the kilts sway
to greet us.
You are the opening,
the gap we streak through
to the woolly wilds
of Auld Reekie
and Bonnie Old Dundee;
to the sea of workers'™ blood,
the red rust of the past that clings
and hugs the bones of dead engineers.
In the Albert Hotel,
tucked up, I hear you moan in the darkness.
Naked,
I pull back the curtains
and see you floodlit

in all your entrancing glory.
Shine on, shine
you crazy bridge.
You have my devotion,
you have my deepest darkest love.
I would climb you stripped;
I would feel you breathe in the Firth wind.
I give you my heart and soul,
I am frail against your depth.
You will outlive me,
do not mock me,
you are superb.
You are my outstretched lovely;
I will breathe through you,
long for you,
die for you.
Rock me,
go Forth
and inspire me.

Keith Armstrong

THE OCCUPIER

Ross stared out of the window. He felt like screaming. Sometimes, at first light, he saw rats gnawing the crusts of bread and chicken bones, chips and bacon rinds that the residents of Churchill House had thrown from their windows. This morning, however, a swirling fog cloaked everything but the tops of distant factories and electricity pylons. What if, Ross wondered, when the fog went, there were no people left?

Grinning at the thought of an empty world, Ross made himself a mug of tea. His eyes were red rimmed. His short, dark hair was tangled. He hadn't shaved for three days. Wild looking, he watched condensation descend the damp-smudged walls.

Would the drip to his left or the drip to his right reach the skirting first?

Ross was too irritable to care. He had been up for hours, sitting at the window, watching dawn ascend the sky, hoping to see rats.

His mind wouldn't shut down and let him sleep. Yet - frustratingly - his thoughts led nowhere, brought no sense of accomplishment or satisfaction.

Wasn't sleeplessness meant to be something that troubled old men?

It was, and that added to his frustration, for Ross was just twenty years old.

Sleeplessness had made him irritable, restless. Too impatient to wait for the kettle, he turned off the gas, left the flat in a hurry.

Ross took the stairs. His black trainers were worn. 'No name trainers,' the local kids called them, pointing and laughing. Cold from the steps penetrated his feet, making them tingle and ache. He let himself out of the back door. Only the caretaker was meant to have a key, but once, when prizing some screaming, lager-soaked soul from the lift, the caretaker had made the mistake of placing his toolbox and master key on the floor behind him. Grunting with the effort, throwing the full weight of his fleshy body against the crow bar, the caretaker hadn't seen or heard Ross, had just discovered, some fifteen minutes later, that his master key was gone. The caretaker was in his late fifties. His hair was white. His cheeks were a mass of broken veins. He looked worn out. Ross didn't hate him, didn't want him to die, though he badly wanted his job. Stealing the master key had been part of that. If there had been more time he would have stolen tools, too.

The fog reeked of sewage, was so cold it stung his cheeks and fingertips. Crossing the car park Ross noted the abandoned car, its windscreen smashed, its stereo ripped out, seatbelts hanging from the doors like the intestines of a gutted cow.

Breathing through his teeth, trying to rub warmth into his fingers, he crossed Staines Road.

He started running as soon as he reached the towpath.

Scrap yards and abandoned factories rushed at him. The canal itself stank of poisonous chemicals, though the factories had been empty for decades, their owners escaped to swimming pool lives. Here and there pus-yellow scum coated the surface of the water and protruding from it were prams, car tyres, bobbing Coke cans. Ross saw the water-bloated body of a dead kitten and dozens of glassy-eyed fish.

Quickly drained by the sight of dead things, Ross focused on the towpath. Though his chest was raw from running, life was better when he started to sweat.

Chased hard by the crunch of gravel, slim, blue-eyed, dressed in a back track suit, in a voice that was breathy and frail, he sang: *Welcome To My World,* trying to imitate Jim Reeves' style.

This was the song his dad had sung after he had beaten his mom to death with a pickaxe handle. Though only six years old, Ross remembered her screams and an explosion of blood...

A trigger, the song released more memories:

He recalled, a decade later, his solicitor's plea to the court on a rainy afternoon in June:

The boy saw his mother beaten to death, the solicitor said.

Ross watched his solicitor intently. Saw how he hooked his thumbs into his pinstriped waistcoat. Heard how he spoke - like a bad actor rehearsing his lines, measuring each pause, yet feeling nothing.

Standing in the dock in the only shirt he owned, Ross had lowered his head, gripped by a sense of shame - not for stealing cars, rather for having done nothing to help save his mother. He had been only six. What could he have done? He didn't know. But he wished he had done...something.

The magistrate mistook his personal anguish for public remorse and was lenient. But when he appeared before her again, less than two months later, she demanded to know why he had re-offended.

His solicitor had tried to speak for him - thumbs hooked into the pocket of his waistcoat in readiness.

But the magistrate had held up her hand.

Let him answer! The magistrate demanded, and waited for him to do so, her angry little eyes peering at him from above her spectacles.

Ross had shrugged.

What the fuck do you want? He had asked, looking first at the magistrate, then at his solicitor, and finally at the faces in the gallery.

It all seemed a long time ago and Ross was glad. After forty minutes of running, he was tired. His hands wedged firmly onto his knees, he fought for breath. The fog had thinned. Lactic acid burned in his thighs, yet, reaching Churchill House, he decided to slog up the ten flights of stairs rather than take the lift.

'You must be mad,'Karen said.

She sat in front of the TV, her gaze flitting between him and the on screen images.

Sweating, Ross sat next to her. With his thumb he traced the frown lines in his forehead. To be mad was to be off-kilter. Unbalanced. Insane. To say that he was mad, even if it was meant as a joke, wounded him. Why didn't she know that? Why couldn't she read his mind? He wished she could. For there were many things he wanted to say to her and couldn't. It felt as if he were blocked up. As if the inside of his head was a cupboard filled with the debris of many lifetimes. The door to the cupboard was locked and he didn't have the key. Not even the master key he had stolen from the caretaker of Churchill House would open it. I love you, was one of the things he wanted to say. But his tongue wouldn't move. Might have been glued to the base of his mouth. He put his arm around Karen's shoulders. That he loved her would, he hope, be communicated through his touch.

'You're all sweaty!'Karen said, recoiling.

She had fucked half the lads in Year Eleven, she had told him, the achievement described with deliberation and in great detail. But she chose to live with him. He had been selected.

'Do you want some breakfast?'he asked, standing, wanting to repay her for selecting him and not one of the others.

Karen didn't answer, engrossed by a weather report.

'You ought to eat something.'

Karen was three months pregnant - exactly the duration of his impotence.

If I get desperate - Karen had told him after their most recent attempt - I'll look up one of my Year Elevens! Danny Thomas's hung like a donkey!

She had laughed, the sound like cold water poured onto a hot pan.

When Ross didn't join in Karen had assured him she was: Only joking! After which she had left him to view the knobbly protrusions of her spine.

Breaking his train of thought, Karen said:

'Hark at you! You sound just like my mom.'

How could that be? For her mom had left when Karen was three - had run off with a man who taught disco dancing above a fish and chip shop on Benbury High Street. Since he could barely remember what his own mom looked like, much less things she had said - and he had been twice Karen's age when he last saw her - Ross didn't believe this was Karen's memory. She stole things from TV, repeating them as if they were part of her real life. Ross might have pursued this, but the letterbox flapped open and he turned sharply.

Since he had learned of the pregnancy he had been applying for jobs in earnest.

His search for employment had taken him first to the job centre. There a pale, ginger-haired man had asked him what other jobs he'd had.

Never had a job, Ross had replied.

The ginger-haired man had written something down. Then he had asked Ross what kind of thing he was interested in. He wasn't interested in anything, Ross told the ginger-haired man.

Skills? The man had raised his eyebrows, his pen poised, expectant.

I just want a job, Ross had told him, his chest practically touching the man's desk - everything orderly on it, every pencil freshly sharpened.

A training course had been offered. Ross had shaken his head. He had tried a training course once before, when he first got out of remand.

The people running the course smiled all the time, as if everything they said was really a joke, but only they got why it was funny:

You have to sell yourself to an employer - said with a smile...

I want you to write down five positive things about yourself - said with an even bigger smile...

Ross had tried to think of five things. He would have settled for four things, three things, anything. His head was pounding. The way it used to when Kelvin - the daddy in his remand home - had been to see him, using his head as a punch bag because the screws wouldn't let him into the gym, wouldn't let him use any of the boxing equipment.

No offence, Kelvin said.

WHAP!

(A left to the head.)

You see?

WHAP!

(A right to the head.)

I've got to stay in shape.

WHAP!

(Left.)

Or I won't be the daddy anymore.

WHAP!

(Right.)

You see how it is, don't you?

WHAP! WHAP! WHAP!

(Left, right, left.)

On the sheet of lined paper he had been given, his head ready to explode, Ross had finally written: I JUST WANT A FUCKING JOB.

No courses, he had told the ginger-haired man. I want a real job, with wages, so I can support my girlfriend and my kid when it's born.

Since then Ross had been sending out application forms. He had no skills. No experience. But he was willing to work. I WILL WORK HARD was something he wrote on all the application forms he completed.

But there were no offers that morning. Just a brown envelope addressed to: The Occupier, which he tore open in the hallway.

Churchill House was one of three ten-storey flats comprising Kendal Rise. The residents of Churchill House, McMillan, and Eden House were to be re-homed, said the letter. Urban renewal, it said. Noting that the flats were to be empty by November the first, Ross crumpled the letter into his pocket and returned to the Lounge. Karen was still watching TV - watching it with real concentration, as if she was to be tested on what she had seen. The run had calmed him, but the calmness now gave way to his familiar jumpiness. It felt like his head was swarming with angry ants. What were they angry about?

'Shush!'Her eyes riveted to the screen, like a schoolteacher Karen held her forefinger against her lips.

'What?'

Had he spoken? Had he inadvertently said something about the demolition of Churchill House? The frown lines carved into his forehead deepened. Ross looked worried and old - nearer forty than twenty, a man at the end of his tether, pale, shrunken, defeated.

'That tune,'Karen said, her eyes widening with pleasure when a woman in purple ski pants charged into her boyfriend - who had just told the audience that he had been having affairs with her younger sister and her mother.

Ross made a fist of his right hand and pressed it against his forehead. This did nothing to lessen the frenzied work of the ants inside his skull.

'That Jim Reeves thing you're always humming,' she continued. 'I don't even know who he is. Is Jim Reeves your hero or something?'

*

Ross wore a green shirt, an overcoat with a broken zipper, black jeans and his 'no name' trainers. That morning he had shaved and carefully brushed his hair. Still he looked wild, his eyes unsettled and unsettling, anxious and angry. Earlier he had made himself a cheese sandwich; had buried it in half a metre of kitchen foil. Now he took it from his pocket and unwrapped it. From a distance Ross looked like a man trying to launch a metallic kite. The interview was at eleven. He had twenty minutes to kill, so though he wasn't hungry, he ate his sandwich, swallowing after barely chewing, staring off at the choppy surface of the lake.

The letter telling of the demolition was in his pocket. Now three weeks old, it was badly crumpled, but when he had finished eating Ross reread it. Of course nothing had changed, yet somehow he kept expecting that it would. If I get the job, he decided, I'll tell Karen about the letter. To do so at that point made sense. A new job and a new home went well together.

His hands jammed into his pockets, Ross circumnavigated the lake, restless, twitchy. Karen had said he should see a doctor. Get some medication to calm his nerves. Running is my medication, he had said.

Near the overgrown island at the centre of the lake Ross saw a boat. Its broken belly was full of sludge-grey water. How long had it been there? Who owned it? Biting into his bottom lip stopped him singing or humming *Welcome To My World.*

Heath Park smelled of rotten meat. The grass was drowning in dew and the outstretched arms of the trees were stark against the white sky - as if they were begging.

Though some minutes still remained before the interview, Ross started walking, a man intent on confronting his destiny.

No skills required, the advert stated. He hadn't even had to complete an application form. If he proved successful in his interview, they would do the necessary paperwork the woman he had telephoned had said.

Ms Shakespeare was Head of Personnel at Brannon's, a store selling everything from garden tools to toothpicks, and cheaply. Someone was needed to unload deliveries. A strong back was what they wanted, and Ross had that.

Walking up the grassy incline from the lake with his head down and his hands stuffed into his pockets, Ross felt optimistic, the inside of his chest warm, his breathing easy. Why shouldn't he get this job? He was fit, he was strong, and he was willing to work.

Blinkered by his optimism, Ross failed to see the two men lurking by the trees defining the perimeter. Both men had tattooed skulls. Both wore very tight fitting faded blue jeans.

'Give us your money you fucker!'

The smaller of them was a head taller than him, with red, butcher-boy hands. Ross didn't like fighting - had no talent for it, this something he had learned at the remand home when Mr Cole insisted he take part in the evening of boxing being staged for the governor and the governor's guests.

What do you weigh? Mr Cole had asked.

Ross had told him.

A light-welter...that's good, Mr Cole had said

The fight had taken place in a makeshift ring whose ropes hung loose. It had lasted less than a minute. Broken by the first punch thrown, Ross's nose had showered blood over the governor and the governor's guests.

You're absolutely fucking useless! Mr Cole had yelled, his disgust and his spittle prolific.

Ross would have run from the tattooed men. But they were too close, so he told them - truthfully - that he had on him only eighty-nine pence - less than his bus fare home.

'You lying little shit!'

'I'm serious, I-'

*

Ms Shakespeare was twenty-three years old. Her forehead was high and prematurely lined. Though her eyesight was not weak, she wore spectacles, feeling they gave her more authority. That she didn't suffer fools gladly and worked hard were two of her most prized features. The third was that she was able, so she believed, to control her face.

However, when first she set eyes on Ross her mouth inadvertently opened and her eyes widened and bulged. Only when she regained her usual composure did Ms Shakespeare gesture for him to take a seat. She refrained from asking him what had happened.

'I've got a strong back,' Ross said. He was nervous. It was in his voice and his smile.

There was blood on his teeth, she saw, gathering each detail to recount later.

'That's good,' she said. Normally, she liked to greet a candidate with a barrage of questions, but now her head felt empty.

'I can work hard,' Ross said, taking her silence as his cue. His face felt stiff. There was dried blood at the corners of his mouth and his left eye was starting to blacken and swell. He had done well to limit the damage, but then he knew how to minimize the effects of a beating. Protect your head at all costs was the golden rule, and with the skinheads in Heath Park he had done just that, taking punishment to his face only as he went down.

Cursing, the skins had kicked him as if he were an enormous football. If the goalposts hadn't been stolen they might have kicked him through them. Finally, exhausted by their exertions, they had stopped. One of them had knelt, had reached into his pockets, and had taken out his money and the letter addressed to: The Occupier. When the skins had gone Ross had seen the letter in the dew soaked grass. Had picked it up. Dried it with his hands. Pushed it back into his coat pocket.

'And I can work long,' Ross added. Then he sucked in air and gave Ms Shakespeare everything...He told her about his dad, and his mom, and the remand home. Of never having had a job. Of Karen and the baby and the letter from the council. (At this point he took it from his pocket and unfolded it - creased and wet as a cabbage leaf, so that Ms Shakespeare could see it.) Finally, Ross repeated that he had a strong back and that he could work long and hard.

'I just need a chance to show it,' he concluded.

Ms Shakespeare knew it was her turn to speak but, still taken aback, she could only blink. There were various papers on her desk. To buy herself some time she straightened them.

'Thank you.' She raised the corners of her mouth.

'Have I got the job?' Ross noticed there was mud on his trousers. If he had seen it earlier he would have scraped it off.

'I can start tomorrow.' He squared his shoulders. 'I can start now if you want me to.'

It was policy at Brannon's to keep paperwork to a minimum by informing candidates of the outcome of their interview immediately. The only other candidate for the post was forty and, with a long history of spinal disk problems, had, until now, seemed less than ideal.

'I'm afraid I have disappointing news for you-' Ms Shakespeare began.

Before she could go further, close to tears, Ross stood up, gripped by disappointment, rage and frustration.

'Why?'

He had been dirtied; his left eye was closing; his mouth was full of blood. He hadn't lived a perfect life - that he had confessed, but now Ross wanted a chance to show he could do more than fuck up.

'P-please,' he stammered.

'The decision has been made,' Ms Shakespeare said, as if she were not responsible for making it, 'and it is irreversible.' She came from behind her desk, heading for the door, opening it smoothly, intent on ushering him out.

Ross looked at her then at the open door. The ants inside his head were on the march and Jim Reeves was close by - he could hear him singing *Welcome to My World*, the same line over and over again: a stuck record.

Shut the fuck up, Jim! Was one of the things Ross wanted to say, and he opened his mouth to say it -

The next thing he remembered was being back at the flat, Karen by his side, the two of them painted a mottled orange by the glow from the electric fire.

'Is there something you want to tell me?' Karen said. Her arms were folded. Her hair crackled with static electricity.

Ross licked his lips. Swallowed. His mouth still tasted of dried blood. His eye was almost closed, but the pain had receded. He reached into his pocket to touch the letter. Then sharply withdrew his fingers.

'No,' Ross said, ready to look away if she turned towards him.

Karen laughed.

'I was talking to the TV,' she said. 'I've seen this before,' she explained, pointing, 'and that's what he says next.'

'Is there something you want to tell me?' said the man on the TV.

'Told you,' Karen said, rocking with mirth, oblivious to the tears flowing from Ross' uninjured eye.

*

That night Ross dreamt he was in a swamp, lost and alone, the black mud sucking him under, the pressure against his chest enormous. Panicked, he sat up, his heart beating erratically.

Karen was still asleep when he pulled on his tracksuit and padded from the bedroom.

He turned on the radio. Seated on the floor he listened to a caller extolling the virtues of the birch. If you birched offenders, the caller said, it taught them a lesson they never forgot. Hanging and flogging should be brought back. Then the prisons wouldn't be overcrowded!

After a few minutes, sickened, Ross turned off the radio. His head still hurt and though he hadn't examined his body he could feel where the men in Heath Park had kicked him, his chest, back and thighs a patchwork quilt of bruises.

This patchwork quilt Ross took out of the flat and up onto the roof of Churchill House.

Night winds tugged at his hair and riffled his tracksuit. He let himself into the laundry. The washing and drying machines - unused for many years - looked dead. He trailed his fingertips over the flat-cool surfaces before going back outside. From his pocket he took the letter. A new job, a new home, and a new life...those things had been possible only a few hours ago.

Then everything had changed.

Was he going to let them relocate him?

By way of answer, his eyes glistening with anger, sorrow and resolve, Ross opened his fingers and let the wind take the letter from him - dancing it up and away.

*

Karen gave him two days.

All the others wanted to fuck her and forget her. Which had been okay when she was fourteen and gathering scalps. But when she reached eighteen it was time to find someone who would stay around, who would support her. Convinced that one out of two wasn't bad, she had decided to settle for Ross.

They had met in The Stag. He was, her friend Julie told her, just out of remand. Lived in a one bedroom flat in Churchill House. Had no family to mess things up. Liked to drink when he had some money, but didn't do drugs. Was, according to Anne-Marie Stack, who had sampled the goods: a fairly decent fuck.

Karen had moved herself into Ross' flat after she had twice tried him herself. He wasn't the best she'd had, but Anne-Marie Stack wasn't wrong, and, more important than his rating - 6/10 - was that he didn't give her any of the usual shit about not being ready to commit, not being ready to settle down. Ross was quiet. He let her choose which channel they watched on TV. (He promised her when he got a job, he would get a satellite dish installed.) Love didn't come into it, but Karen did like him.

When, the day after his beating Ross wasn't there, Karen thought nothing of it. He was often out running when she woke.

But when he hadn't returned by lunchtime, by early afternoon, by evening, Karen knew something was wrong.

The bastard's up and left me! she decided. She knew how that felt because Leroy had done the same thing. They had been together only nineteen days when Karen woke to find herself alone. The fucker had even taken her best pair of fishnet tights! But that Leroy was a kinky bastard was something Karen knew all about! Leroy left no note, nothing...No, that wasn't quite true. He had left: three months unpaid rent, plus outstanding gas and electricity bills.

That's men for you, Julie told her, the two of them drinking rum and coke, Karen with everything she owned in a sports bag with a broken handle.

Recalling Leroy's departure, Karen checked Ross' things. They were all still there. Would he leave everything? Was that like him? She realised that she didn't know what he was like, not really. Julie had told her more about him than he ever had.

On the second day Karen woke to the sensation that someone had been watching her. Nothing had been moved, yet the feeling that someone had been there with her persisted. More carefully this time, she went through Ross's things. Finding a Jim Reeves tape wrapped inside a pair of jeans, she placed it on the floor and drove her heel into it. A little destruction was good for her soul since for the rest of the day she was content to watch TV as usual, only occasionally looking at the time.

Finally it grew dark and, as if this was a signal, Karen packed and left.

Later, in The Stag, the broken handled sports bag beneath a wrought iron table, drinking Guinness because Julie said it was good for the baby, Karen made it clear she had decided to be philosophical:

'I suppose he always was a bit of a wanker!'

Julie, sucking hard on a cigarette, nodded avidly.

'All men are.'

Twice married and twice divorced, though only twenty-two, Julie was a self-appointed authority on the male.

'Ever since I got pregnant his dick was limp!'

'You're kidding me?'

'No.' Karen stuck out her bottom lip, as if it were evidence.

'You think that's why he pissed off?'

'That or the baby.'

Julie nodded: It fit with her thesis. She lifted her chin and blew out smoke.

'So what're you going to do?'

'I thought I could stay with you for a bit.'

Julie picked flecks of ash from her black skirt.

'I think Gavin's going to be moving in soon.'

'Gavin?'

'I know,'Julie said. 'He's lost his hair and it makes him look older. But he's only twenty-nine - he told me so. Says I can see his birth certificate if I like.'

'What about his kids?'

'Only the boys are his. The girls don't look like him or anything.'

'You said all men are wankers.'

'They are. But Gavin's a mechanic, think how useful that is.'

'I suppose so,' Karen said, fiddling with a beer mat.

Seeing the forlorn look on Karen's face, Julie drained her glass with a flourish.

'Gavin hasn't sorted out his maintenance yet. He won't move in till that's sorted. You can stay till you find somewhere else.'

Karen stood up.

'I'll get these,' she said, relieved, bending to collect their empty glasses from the table. 'Same again?'

'Too fucking right!' Julie said.

At 3AM, his canvas rucksack on his back, Ross came down from the roof. He no longer ran, but each night he walked along the Astbury Road to the hyperstore opposite the Bingo complex half a mile from Benbury, walking with his head down, as if avoiding eye contact on a crowded street, though in fact he rarely passed anyone, and when he did they were usually drunk and weaving, oblivious to him.

The hyperstore, an island in a sea of car parks, was bathed in sodium light. The store was open 24 hours a day, the rattle of trolleys a constant.

Ross made for the rear of the store. A CCTV camera was perched on the end of the wall furthest from the service entrance. Using his peripheral vision, he watched the camera tracking from left to right. When it reached the furthest point of its trajectory he turned suddenly and sprinted. Reaching the top of the wall in a second, Ross dropped into the yard before the camera started its return journey.

The yard was poorly lit. Eight refuse receptacles occupied the space. Since the CCTV camera pointed out not in, it was necessary only to watch the door allowing access to the rear of the bakery. Slipping off his rucksack, Ross approached the nearest receptacle. Standing on tiptoe, he lifted the lid and began to root about inside. The secret was not to dig deep, for stuff that was way down was too damaged, useless. Quickly, he found bread and cakes - his staple diet in his new life. After adding four cartons of apple juice to the rucksack he was about to leave when the door to the main building swung open and a man in white overalls stepped out. The man, no older than he, though taller and heavier, lit a cigarette.

When the man returned to his work, Ross scaled the wall. He waited until the CCTV camera was directed away from him before descending and hurrying across the car park.

Usually, once he had his supplies, Ross returned promptly to Churchill House. But seeing the man in the yard had driven his thoughts back to his old life. These thoughts compelled him to head for the town centre.

The High Street was deserted. Here Ross felt strange, edgy, the way he had been in his old life. The empty shops were threatening, dark secrets lurking in their shadows. Near the end of the High Street, he stopped. The interview at Brannon's had changed things. Like a river deflected by a pebble, his course had been forever altered and now, taking a French loaf from his rucksack, Ross peeled back the cellophane and gave vent to his feelings: Using the loaf as a sort of enlarged crayon, and the pavement as a writing tablet, he wrote: SHAKESPEARE IS A BASTARD, little knowing that later that day the Benbury Chronicle would include a snippet headlined: BENBURY VANDALS ARE ANTI-BARD!

*

On the way to the roof Ross let himself into the flat where he used to live. For the third week there was no post, a sign that the outside world was receding.

He moved stealthily through the darkened rooms, then left: satisfied nothing had been altered, but feeling vaguely troubled.

Always careful, Ross locked the steel door leading to the roof before unpacking the contents of his rucksack. The laundry room contained food and the letters he had taken from his flat - the Department of Social Security demanding to know why he hadn't been to sign on, those addressed to The Occupier informing him, in terms increasingly hostile, that he had to vacate the premises. He opened a tin of beans. Began to spoon them into his mouth, re-reading each letter by the light of the moon. Most of the residents of Churchill House had already left. When everyone was gone, what would he do? This was a question he had asked many times. Always the exactitudes proved elusive, but always he asserted that, come what may, he would remain.

Finished eating, Ross returned to the ground floor. Through the glassed front doors he saw McMillan and Eden House emerging like the legs of a giant from the darkness. Usually, when it got light he went to the laundry, drew over himself the sheets he had taken from the bed he had shared with Karen, and slept the sleep of the innocent until darkness fell. Yet tonight memories of the old life seemed sharper and more persistent than they had for some time. The trip to the High Street was one he wouldn't make again, Ross decided. In the meantime, he wasn't tired. Without really giving it any consideration, he decided to see if he could find Karen.

*

His search that day proved fruitless, but over the following months Ross made several forays into the daylight. Always, he hoped to see Karen, though he had no desire to be seen by her. His hair was now long - it was possible that even if she did set eyes on him she wouldn't recognise him.

Then, on November 2nd, it became necessary, to stop going out altogether. Icy winds tore the last of the leaves from the trees and workmen in blue boiler suits arrived in white Transits. Hands in pockets, nursing hangovers, the workmen clambered clumsily from their vans. After a few minutes the caretaker came out to greet them. The caretaker told the workmen that the last occupant had moved out the night before; that he had spent the night on a camp bed just inside the main doors to make sure nobody came in; that the building was now theirs and they were welcome to it. His duty dispensed, he walked from Churchill House for the last time, carrying his camp bed and a flask; the caretaker didn't look back.

The men in boiler suits passed round cigarettes. When they had finished smoking they dispatched a man to find a café and bring back bacon sandwiches, leaving the rest to take from the rears of their vans rectangles of steel which they affixed, during the course of the morning - pausing only to eat bacon sandwiches, smoke more cigarettes, and flick through newspapers - to the main entrance, the rear entrance, and all the first floor windows of Churchill House, thus securing the building until it was demolished.

When Churchill House was sealed, the men in boiler suits repeated the process, first with McMillan and then with Eden House. At the day's end, shrunk by tiredness but sweat free of their hangovers, the workmen clambered back into their Transits and left.

That night stars glistened and it was bitterly cold, yet Ross lay with his hands behind his head at the centre of the roof. Not long after dark he heard glass being smashed, the sound so loud it made his heart shudder. He moved to the edge of the roof. So long as he didn't lean over the mottled steel fence there was little chance of him being seen. A dozen teenaged boys and girls - dressed in baggy jeans and, despite the cold, tee shirts - concentrated first on finding stones, then on throwing them, leaping with joy whenever they broke glass, converts to the joy of destruction.

In less than an hour the lower windows were gone. Reaching the higher windows required more strength, and better aim, but the destructors persevered

High above them Ross wandered if the police would come.

But apparently no summons was made, for the police didn't arrive and fatigue it was, after almost an hour of frantic throwing, that ended the first assault - leaving behind only silence and a glass moat.

Others stopped to assault the building. For most it was casual: stoop, select a stone, throw it, then move on - actions completed seemingly without thought. But a little before nine two women stopped their car, got out and approached the building with intent. Believing themselves unobserved, they threw hard at the higher windows, screaming with delight when they scored a direct hit and one of the few remaining panes imploded, after which they hurried away, giggling.

The siege continued until after midnight, men and women, young and old, all taking their turn. The final attacker was a white haired man who, drunk and raving, bent, peeled off one of his shoes, and threw it, cursing his life and the planet earth.

*

Having slept fitfully for only two hours, Ross awakened, gulped down water, and then readied himself for the second advance. Surely, now, there would be drilling, hammering, pounding. Then explosive charges would be planted. Which of the buildings would they demolish first? Like buzzards, a multitude of questions circled inside his head. Ross went down from the roof. Through flats full of shattered glass and the detritus of former occupants, he restlessly roamed. His questions, however, sadistic tormentors that they were, refused to release him from their grip.

But that day there was no second advance: The outside world seemed to have lost interest in the sealed, blinded building.

For a week Ross stayed on red alert, hardly sleeping, hardly eating, moving from flat to flat with the restless, crazed grace of a caged tiger. While he waited, and though he freely availed himself of his supplies, Ross grew thinner. The skin beneath his eyes darkened. When would they come? When?

But no one did, and, unbeknownst to Ross, no one would...

Douglas Nichols drove the toe of his patent leather shoe through the air conditioning vent adjacent the entrance to his office.

Though he was just forty-one years old, the act left Nichols breathless. But then he made a habit of drinking coffee until he shook and smoking cigarettes until he coughed. His idea of exercise was to yell at his underlings.

After retrieving his foot - breathing harder still from the effort, the purple veins in his cheeks becoming suffused with blood - Nichols gathered himself to do just that.

As usual, Howard Jackson was to bear the brunt of Nichols' fury.

Nichols pointed at the chrome chair before his desk and commanded his subordinate to:

'Sit.'

Obediently, Jackson sat.

And waited.

Though the same age as Nichols, Jackson looked a dozen years younger, his hair still dark, his complexion clear.

'The air conditioning is fucking useless!' Nichols snapped. 'Minute that,' he added, 'but omit the Anglo-Saxon.'

For Nichols, life was a meeting.

Jackson nodded - he didn't have his notepad with him, but his memory was good.

'It's too hot to breathe in this place! If a man can't breathe, he can't be expected to think straight. Am I right or am I right?'

Nichols sat facing Jackson, sweat rolling down the sides of his face.

'In this heat mistakes are made.'

Studying the dandruff on Nichols' shoulders, Jackson crossed his legs. This would take five minutes. The duration of the outpouring was, Jackson knew, inversely proportional to the degree of his anger: the angrier Nichols was, the shorter the outpouring.

'There's no fucking money left to take down those monstrosities on the Beeches Farm Estate!'

Nichols rummaged through papers on his desk - finally locating the one he wanted.

'Look at this!' he spluttered, thrusting the sheet at Jackson, who took it from him politely, keeping his eyes on Nichols rather than the columns of figures on the sheet in his hand.

'I was elected because of my dynamism, am I right or am I right?' After a coughing fit that darkened his cheeks to the colour of a plum, Nichols thumbed sweat from the corners of his mouth. 'But nobody wants a dynamo who over spends. Who the fuck approved that budget?'

'Would you like me to check?' Jackson raised both his eyebrows.

Nichols clenched his fists. Jackson was efficient, but smarmy.

'No, I don't want you to check!'

Nichols felt like sweeping the papers from his desk in a single, bold gesture. But he refrained and, after a moment, controlling his voice, asked quietly:

'Have all the residents gone?'

'As of last night.'

His anger giving way to resignation, Nichols became conscious that his foot, where he had kicked the air conditioning vent, hurt: a persistent throbbing pain.

'What a fuck up!'

Without moving or speaking, Jackson conveyed to Nichols that, on this point, he was in full agreement.

Nichols' shoulders were hunched. His suit looked like a dishrag.

'Are the buildings sealed?'

Jackson nodded.

'That's good.' Nichols grinned, showing stained teeth. 'In that case we do nothing.' He sat back in his chair, not happy, but working towards a state of satisfaction. 'We don't spend another penny. We leave the buildings where they are, sealed, hurting no one, incurring no more cost.' Eventually, there would be complaints - Nichols envisaged TV interviews with people from the Estate, the word 'eyesore' being repeated, like an echo, images of the three buildings in a provocative state of decay. But by then he would be out of office and far from Benbury. That you could make a mess and not have to clear it up was Nichols favourite thing about politics.

Realising that their meeting was concluded, Jackson stood. Five minutes...As usual he had been bang on, and felt good about it. Little things helped preserve your sanity in a job like his.

'Distribute the minutes widely,' Nichols said, 'but Howard?'

Jackson, reaching for the door handle, turned.

'Edit carefully.'

'Yes, Douglas.'

*

Ross was halfway through his food store when he decided to venture out again. He waited until midnight. From a second floor balcony he studied the pork factory - a pre-fabricated building fronted by iron railings. It ran shifts. Accordingly, the lights were on. The stench was so strong Ross was sure his tongue and throat were coated with meat fat.

Ross climbed the rail. Conscious of the weight of the cable and the steel candelabra, he hung from the bottom of the balcony. Dropping lightly to the ground, he checked the factory. Saw it was not watchful and so, unobserved, set off, turning often to look behind, as if he were being followed, his mind exaggerating the threat posed by the world outside Churchill House. But on the way back from the hyperstore, when his rucksack was so full that the straps cut into his shoulders, Ross relaxed. Beneath a sky full of weeping stars, though he passed broken shops and houses that glared angrily at him, his innards became whisky-warm.

Ross didn't hear the approach of the car. Didn't turn until the vehicle mounted the pavement directly behind him. By which time it was too late to do anything but lurch to his left in a desperate attempt to get clear.

The three boys in the silver Toyota were drunk. Jimmy, the driver, had goaded the other two, telling them they were gutless if they refused to come with him. He had stolen cars before, he told them. The cider had helped persuade them. They had drunk it before they set foot on the gravely car park of the Benbury Working Men's Club, Jimmy brandishing his tool kit, bragging he could get into the car quicker than Max could count to twenty.

Only when they were in the car, Jimmy pushing the steering wheel through his hands the way he had seen it done in the movies, did the cider, cut with adrenalin, start to really kick in.

Jimmy drove fast, wanting to show them what he was capable of. He threw the car around corners, crunched gears, urged Max to feed a tape into the stereo. When Max complied, Jimmy cursed him, and reached forward to yank the tape out. Who was Jim Reeves anyway? Feeling blasted, Jimmy tossed the tape out of the window and started to sing a composite of several songs he liked, moving his head from side to side. Not concentrating on driving, Jimmy failed to see the pothole in the road - on the roadways repair list for almost fifteen months, budget deficits accounting for the fact that it hadn't been fixed.

When the car slammed into the pothole, the steering wheel was wrenched from his fingers. Panic-stricken, Jimmy dug his foot onto the brake. The car skidded. Hit the kerb. Mounted it. Hit something. Finally screeched to a stop.

Max found himself on his hands and knees. Watery-eyed, he began frantically to examine himself for wounds, convinced he was at death's door until he saw Ross by the picket fence fronting Sally's Sandwich Shop.

'You fucking killed him,' Max slurred, pointing.

Stumbling, disoriented, but otherwise unscathed, Jimmy and Alvin made their way to where Max was standing.

'Check his pockets,' Jimmy snapped.

'You serious?'

Max pushed his fingers through his dyed blonde hair.

'I'll do it my fucking self!' Jimmy snapped, pleased with himself: for if he hadn't come up with the idea of sacking the poor dead bastard he might have lost face, a fate worse than death.

Illuminated by the headlights, Jimmy tapped down Ross' pockets.

'Fuck all there!'

'We better go,' Alvin said, turning this way and that to confirm that they were alone.

Jimmy nodded and the three hurried away, weaving slightly as they crossed the road and cut through an alley, heading deeper into the Estate, leaving Ross, stunned since the impact, to stir.

Something hot and wet pressed against his face and the smell of meat washed over him. For several moments, his eyes had been open, yet Ross had been able to see nothing. Now, like an old television warming up, his vision cleared and he saw the hot wet thing was a tongue and that the tongue belonged to a small dog. Though he had never owned one, Ross had always liked dogs, but when the tongue refused to be deterred he grasped the animal by the scruff of the neck. The dog's eyes bulged. Clutching the animal in his right hand, he used his left hand to push his upper body off the ground. His head felt as if it were full of wet sand. His left leg was uninjured. Though it made him drip with sweat, Ross was able to stand. The combined weight of his rucksack and the dog made the muscles on either side of his spine tremble. The world jazz-danced away from him. A car passed by, its exhaust blowing. The car would slow, would stop, Ross was sure of it.

But it didn't.

Ignored, Ross limped, the dog still clutched tightly to him, the pain a writhing thing that attacked without remorse.

By the time he reached Churchill House the pain in his ankle had given way to numbness. He felt light-headed and nauseous. The second floor balcony was just a few feet above him, yet it looked unreachable. Ross was gripped by a futile, energy-sapping anger, but that quickly gave way to despair. He was ready to cry. Expected tears to flow. Was therefore surprised to hear laughter instead. Without hope, without expectation, everything was funny if you wanted it to be and Ross wanted it to be. Standing crookedly beneath the balcony, dripping sweat, he shook with laughter for several minutes.

After which he hobbled back a pace and saw he was still holding the dog. He hadn't meant to kill it.

'I'm sorry,' he whispered, and placed it on the ground.

Like a snake shedding its skin, Ross freed himself from his rucksack. Sweat gummed his unruly hair to his face. He searched for the candelabra and cable. The muscles on either side of his spine were fibrillating again. He wanted to fill his lungs with clean air, to exorcise the nausea, but his chest felt constricted. His strength was fading by the minute. If he didn't act soon, he would be too weak to do anything but lie down. He would slip into unconsciousness. Would awake in a hospital. Institutions reeked of pent up lives. Ross hated and feared their rules, their questions. Fuelled by this fear he threw the makeshift grappling hook once, twice, three times before he succeeded in snagging the balcony. He drew his rucksack back on. Desperation tightened his throat. He reached high - and grasped the cable. Immediately his arms trembled. Yet he pulled, and slowly, like a phoenix from the ashes, rose from the chewing gum-stained concrete.

Finally, Ross reached the balcony. Gripping the cool rail with both hands, he hauled his left leg up, and straightened his thigh, the long, curved quadriceps muscle quivering.

In raising it, clumsy, fatigued, his right foot struck the rail. Thus rudely awakened, the pain roared. He gasped. The weight of his rucksack dragged at him. He sucked air through clenched teeth. The air tasted of blood.

But as the minutes passed the pain quietened, began to grow sleepy. Moving slowly, Ross pulled the cable up after him.

He entered the flat through the balcony doors, remembering to close them behind him. Laughter bubbled from him again. Rang like a discordant bell until he fell forwards into blackness...

His throat was hot and parched. His tongue felt thick. How long had he been out? Was it late afternoon or early morning? It could be either, for a thick grey light hung above him like a shroud. Physically, Ross felt smaller. Shrunken. But he wasn't ready to die! He flexed his fingers, then the toes of his left foot. Below his right ankle he could feel nothing. He dragged himself to the edge of the room. There he struggled to sit upright, eventually propping himself against the wall. His chin was almost resting on his chest. Breathing through loose, swollen lips, Ross removed his rucksack, laid it upon his upper thighs, undid the cool metal catches, began to rummage. One of the milk cartons had burst. He threw it splashingly aside. Another, though twisted out of shape, was not breeched. With trembling, grimy fingers he tore it open. The milk had separated, but he drank it anyway, the sourness driving away the bitter taste of blood. He closed his eyes. How did he feel? Like shit! Yet the milk had helped. His resilience was a comfort.

Shoving his rucksack away, Ross drifted off to sleep, dreaming that he was a child again - alone in a blue room. In the dream he knelt beside a fortress and soldiers. Then things got weird. Now, still dreaming, he was fully-grown and the soldiers were singing a Jim Reeves song. He opened his mouth, ready to scream...

When Ross swam from the dream he saw, just inches away, the face of the dog he had left outside.

In a series of jerks, Ross sat upright.

'I thought you were dead.'

For a moment Ross was convinced the voice was his own - that he was talking about the dog. Then he saw the children - their outlines discernible against the windowed sky.

*

'He was dead!'

This voice belonged to the other boy, taller and slimmer than the first.

By nodding, the boy who had spoken first gave Ross to understand he accepted this.

Ross licked his lips. They tasted of ash, and the dog's meaty breath.

'But he's not dead, now,' the first boy said, hands in pockets, chewing rapidly, his eyes fixed on Ross.

'No,' agreed the second boy.

They were seven or eight years old, hard-eyed kids from the estate.

Should he tell them to go away? Or be nice? Ross could see they were in no hurry to leave.

'You were dead,' the first boy said, stepping closer, speaking quietly, as if in church.

Ross nodded.

'I told him,' the second boy said, kneeling to stroke the dog.

Some biscuits were adrift in his rucksack. Ross tossed them onto the floor. The dog dipped its head and vacuumed them up as he struggled to unscrew the cap from a bottle of orange and pineapple squash.

'You want some help?'

They would take the squash and run Ross was sure, yet he held the bottle out anyway.

The boy screwed off the cap and then, almost as if he were bowing, handed it back.

'He needs water with it,' the first boy piped up.

Ross waited. He was prepared to drink the squash undiluted, but the prospect of cool water made him lick his lips expectantly.

'There's a kitchen through that door-' he used his thumb to gesture.

The taller of the boys left the room and Ross heard the gush of running water.

'How'd you do it? Come back to life, I mean,' the boy persisted.

'Can you keep a secret?'

'I don't grass!' the boy said, raising his chin.

Ross smiled.

'The truth is: I don't know. All I know is: coming back to life is tiring!'

The taller boy returned, having filled a cracked glass vase, explaining this was the only container he could find.

'That's great,' Ross said, taking the vase in both hands and drinking thirstily, adding that - in his opinion - it was a mug fit for a king, which seemed to please both boys and, if its tail was anything to go by, the dog.

Initially, he wanted the boys to leave, but the feeling evaporated. Ross had changed. He felt mentally stronger. The boys seemed to find pleasure in everything he said. Was his life so funny? Maybe. The burning in his throat was gone. He needed to piss. But first he listened to the taller of the boys telling how they had found the dog outside Churchill House. It had shaken itself, stood up, and started yapping. Seeing its excitement they had followed it around to the front of the building. The dog had pawed frenziedly at a rectangular iron cover. Working together the boys had lifted it. The dog had leapt down a short concrete throat and ran along a sloping tunnel to the basement. It had led them to him. He was dead when they found him. Then he rose from the dead. (The shorter boy interrupted to tell how he had seen another dead body - this one pulled from the quarry off Longshanks Road one rainy Sunday afternoon. The body had been as pale as Ross, though not as hairy. There had been cuts along the length of both arms, as if the man - before he drowned - had played noughts and crosses on his body with a razor blade.)

Both boys were seated cross-legged on the floor. At Ross' invitation they ate from the rucksack.

'We'll need to bring the others,' the taller boy said.

Ross fingered his hair back from his face. The numbness in his right ankle gave way to a pulsing ache. He considered telling the boys that he didn't want to see anyone. But they could show up anyway - without his blessing - and he could do what? Hobble after them? Hurl abuse? Besides which he felt comfortable around them. Like a magician, he opened his hands. No doves flew from Ross's palms, yet the boys responded as if they had witnessed a miracle. They stood. The dark was thick as mud.

'Okay,' Ross said, realising only after he had spoken that they had already gone.

He probed his ankle. The flesh felt thick, alien to his fingers, but the skin wasn't punctured. Keeping his back against the wall, he hauled himself erect. The darkness spiralled. He thought he would fall. But, breathing through gritted teeth, and pressing his hands against the wall - like Samson - Ross remained upright. The darkness steadied and, the pressure on his bladder driving him, Ross hopped to the bathroom.

His urine had about it a wounded smell. Yet it wasn't the smell of defeat. He ran cold water through his fingers. Splashed it onto his face and his ankle. When it was light, he intended to bathe the wound properly. Now, he was too tired to do anything, but return to the living room.

He lay down. Never had he felt so tired. Ross closed his eyes. Focused on his heartbeat. Slipped into a deep and - this time - dreamless sleep.

*

Ross woke suddenly, squinting against morning light. Gasping when he saw that the room was full of boys, he sat up.

Moving slowly, the taller of the boys from the previous night took a step forwards.

'We said we'd come back with others.'

'You did,' Ross acknowledged.

'They didn't believe us.'

The boy fidgeted from one foot to the other.

'Do they believe you now?'

The boy turned to survey the faces of the others, dressed like him: in combat trousers, hooded sweat tops, trainers.

'They said you were dead and you came back to life,' a boy to his right spoke up, punctuating his sentence by jabbing his hands ferociously into his pockets.

Ross had always studied people, doing so in order to mimic them. He had acquired a multitude of stances, postures, ways of moving. But his mimicry hadn't had the desired effect for it hadn't ever made him fit in. Ironically, it had served to emphasize the unease he felt about himself, which had accentuated the antagonism his very existence aroused in others. Always Ross had been uncomfortable inside his own skin - until now.

'This,' Ross replied, shaking himself free of his reverie, 'is my second life.'

His words were neither: a joke or a lie.

'Are you sure you're not just a tramp?'

This from: a boy almost directly in front of Ross, a boy who lisped.

Before responding Ross paused to examine his injured ankle. His eyes confirmed what his fingers had deduced the previous night: that no splintered bone had punctured the flesh, and that was good, for there was less likelihood of infection. The flesh itself, though, was bloated and purple. Focusing finally on the lisping boy's question (Perhaps more a challenge than a question) Ross said:

'Do I look like a tramp to you?'

He expected the boy to say: Yes. Instead the boy moved closer. His scrutiny was intense and unashamed. Ross felt as if he was being examined prior to an operation. Yet he didn't flinch.

'No,' said the boy. And meant it. The boy had looked carefully at tramps when he walked though the town centre - at their faces and their eyes. This man's eyes were brighter than a movie star's - and those bright eyes looked right into him. Had he been able to explain it, the boy would have told Ross that his eyes made him feel as if he could never have any secrets from him. It wasn't an uncomfortable feeling. As a matter of fact it made him feel relaxed, at peace. If he had been more perceptive he would have seen from the others' faces that he wasn't alone in this. As it was he added: 'You don't look like a tramp.' Deferentially, the boy stepped back and bowed his head.

Ross was taken aback. For a moment he held his silence. Straightening his spine like a soldier on parade, he said, simply:

'Thank you,' addressing his thanks to them all.

'That's okay,' said the taller of yesterday's visitors - Moses Francis. 'We came back to help.'

As if it were something they had rehearsed, the boys nodded in unison. After sucking his lower lip into his mouth, Moses Francis shrugged.

'Just tell us what to do.'

Ross could see that the boys were serious, their offer made without subterfuge.

'Alright,' he said...

EPILOGUE

Thomas Francis, telephone engineer and single parent, noticed the change in his son almost immediately: Moses seemed older, quieter: not so feisty, not so in his face, more considerate, yet preoccupied. Several times

Thomas said as much to the boy, adding - usually - that this was what growing up was about.

For a time, Thomas approved of the changes, and showed his approval by adding extra fish fingers or sausages to the boy's plate. But pretty soon Thomas felt excluded from his son's life. Always the boy was out. That he should be out with his friends was, Thomas assured himself, normal.

Lord knows I was never in when I was his age, Thomas told Myra, his sometime stay over girlfriend.

Nothing could be more normal, Myra agreed.

Thomas nodded, but still something troubled him. It wasn't so much that Moses was always out: rather that he seemed to have about him such a sense of purpose. When he was Moses' age, Thomas had often been listless. His daddy used to cuss him for it. Moses used to be that way, too.

But not any more...Now when he got in from school, just as smooth as butter Moses changed out of his school uniform, got himself a bite to eat and went straight out.

Right there was something else that bothered Thomas... the eating... Moses was tall, and skinny - literally as thin as a rake. Yet he ate like a horse. However much food Thomas brought in, a day later the cupboards were empty. Thomas asked his son if he were feeding his friends, if they were all coming round to the house after school - whilst he was still at work, asking in such a way as to make clear to Moses that if this was the case he wouldn't be angry. (Though if it turned out to be the case, Thomas intended to suggest it shouldn't be such a one-sided thing, that maybe Moses' friends should invite him to eat at their house from time to time, just to be fair!) But Moses told Thomas he came home alone. Fixed a sandwich to tide him over till teatime, then went out. Moses asked if that was okay.

It had been almost four years since Cherry left. She had taken off with a supermarket manager. The manager had money. Cherry seemed to feel this was an adequate explanation. Maybe it was. Maybe if Thomas had been a better earner she would not have left. He would still have had a wife and Moses would still have had a mother - instead of just a father who nagged him about how much he ate! Thomas said of course it was okay. He checked his nagging, but the feeling that something was amiss remained. How could a boy eat so much and still be so skinny? Was it drugs? A heroin baggie was cheaper than twenty cigarettes and the dealers sold to anyone. That drugs were a possibility made Thomas Francis feel sick. He managed to convince himself, though, that drugs were not responsible. He looked into his son's eyes and saw clarity and purpose - though the nature of the purpose continued to elude him.

It's best you let it go, Myra, told him, and, reluctantly, Thomas was inclined to agree.

Few of the parents of the other eleven boys noticed any real difference in their sons - even the parents of Darren Campbell, the most zealous of the disciples. Their packed lives forced these parents to dole out their love with their eyes half closed. Theirs were lives lived without reflection, lives lived under the premise that if no one was complaining, then nothing was wrong.

Thus it was that the other eleven boys went quietly about their lives.

Thus it was that the boys' daily pilgrimages to Churchill House went undetected.

Even the work they did went unnoticed for the most part. The moat of broken glass remained around Churchill House. But no more litter accrued. The area surrounding the base of the building was neater, tidier, in fact than it had been when the building was fully occupied. There were no food scraps. No dog shit. Mysteriously, the graffiti that had scarred the building vanished.

No one was witness to the cleaning. Yet a few were aware - albeit it subconsciously - that, like a beacon, Churchill House seemed to light up the landscape. The sight of Churchill House - glimpsed as they drove or walked past it, enervated these few.

It went further than that: Men and women, young and old, found themselves - unaccountably - smiling, their anger and anxiety dissipated. Almost imperceptibly the few became many and they began passing Churchill House quite consciously, pausing to look over, not sure why, only that, afterwards, they felt better.

Incidences of local violence fell.

The following spring daffodils rose around Churchill House and for the first time no one tore up the flowers and the scent of fresh growth spread.

Speaking to his only son as spring turned to summer, Thomas Francis said:

'Are you alright? I mean really?'

Looking his father in the eye, Moses nodded.

'I'm better than alright. We all are.'

Thomas held his son's gaze.

'Do you believe me?'

The purpose Thomas had seen in his son's eyes was still there, but the sight of it no longer troubled him.

'I believe you,' Thomas said.

Moses smiled.

'I'm glad,' he said.

Wayne Dean-Richards

Man in Armchair Waiting

1

he thought when you die will you know
what happened to your shadow and where
it had fallen maybe molecules had been shifted
and everywhere the universe could have been
infinitesimally influenced by the passing
of an antelope's shadow over a bare rock

how ridiculous
to think
this way
beauty is the complex
made simple
would this late frost dispel the enthusiasm
of percy evans next door for sowing seeds
this early while wheezing like an exhausted
hippopotamus over his dibbing stick when
he'd be better employed in making his peace
with the landlady of the only pub within a mile

and though
birds
can fly
to water
mules can't

when a sea is raised by a great storm far off
at the other side of an ocean because the waves
are so long you only really take notice of it
when it piles itself on the shore with a voice
of thunder and each roller vents its frustration
against an island spewed from its very mother

a wave   is a wave   is a wave
         is a wave   is a wave
sitting smoking in the chair with a prospect of nothing
things from the other direction would keep catching him up

and passing and it was hard to hold them and all the sounds
for an instant without considering a paradox or two
and eventualities that might be fated by stubbing out a fag
truth is a cloud
clouds obscure

2
as if pushed by an imperceptible wind
the chair would appear
to sail towards a wall of books
and to where an ancient Aztec god
squatted with a scream in its mouth
if he peered very intently
he could see through the books
and beyond that particular god
but it was foggy outside with water
defying gravity and concealing
the mysteries and the face of the clock
was hidden that would chime
the hour of death
he was amused by the tranquility
of all this in comparison
with the waves of frenzy and despairing
boredom that had finally marooned him
on the chair

life's a bobbin of thread
that only knows too well
how to weave itself
into undoable knots
was his current conclusion
he resisted the wayward urge
to get out of the armchair to kiss
the bald head of the god
that screamed silently in order
to discover its reaction to indignity
the chair sailed on

3

another dead day
like a worn-out horse
even the wind plain out of breath
he thought
but all the thinking
didn't stir a leaf
though it conjured mold
and aged flesh
with the stink of pestilence
charred smoke

time ran slow
to speed it up
he shut his eyes dreamed up
a gorge of tumbling rain
imprisoned in dark walls of quartz
so that it spouted an angry roar
but soon its rhythm drugged his ears
eroded the sharpest rocks
and the mist that rose
from the fall muffled
the torrent's tumult
and once more
time sped by
like a loaded hearse

the clock on the wall
was a gaping yawn

4

turning his head to glance over his shoulder
he was surprised
to see a young man diving into green/blue sea
and emerge
with a huge conch shell and within its lustre

a single claw
crouched in the cleft of the nacre-lined abyss
and he knew
that the young man would take the creature
into his boat
crack a hole in the shell near the top with
a machete
poke a thin knife into the hole and evict
the inhabitant
beat it flat with a stick and cut it in pieces
to bait
his hooks for the luring of gold-finned fish

feeling his neck begin to stiffen reluctantly
he left
the young man to gut, scale, garnish and cook
his catch
and looked forward to whatever might appear
on the telly

5
on dozing off
the ketch slid lapping
through the seas the breeze
set steady for the night he steered
sou-west-by south
laying the bowsprit
on a rising star

the star he knew
may well have died
before the dinosaurs had had
their day still floated there
a winking ghost
for him to steer by
for an hour or so

the thought
of those dead stars up there
so saddened him
until above the wave-scape
poked
the bald head of the moon
to lay a silver streak
to white the sails

the full music
of the sky and sea
thrummed in the air
time danced
to the moon's beat
soft wind's flute
under
the carousel of stars

sou-west-by-south
and sailing full and by

6

one night when there was nothing
he could stand to watch on the box
and his brain could only discover cul-de-sacs
he became aware of how the room was turning
very gently
became aware of the world's rolling
and the rhythm of its dance
and the galaxy became intimate
and he wandered
through luminescent clouds of burst stars
peering into black holes
shielding his eyes from an infinity
of suns and swore he could hear
faint as a far cataract
the chant of time and the strings
of its orchestra

7

sallow mornings with the dunking of biscuits
in cooling coffee and drawling towards uneasy
afternoons while the true light only glowed
in evenings where some gladness lurked and
nights that let stars in through the ceiling

but occasionally in the breaking of days
and with dew on his eyelids
all sorts of things would flit around
in the pink light and frightened shadows
then he could laugh and weep for all lovers
and companions without the inhibitions
of true wakefulness
until all the escaped shadows crowded
back round his chair
round his sprawled existence
his methodical dunking of digestives

but a wonder of it could be that
though very conscious of grayness
the steaming coffee would sometimes swirl
into the ever-black sheen of her hair
and a golden sun light on her lips
and her laughter and her skin could
be so soft and yet ivory when
a full moon boldly smiled
and her eyes widened
with amorous agreement

we'll leave him there

Milner Place

Milner Place interviewed by Ian Parks

IP: Milner, I'd like to begin with the long poem. Anyone familiar with your work will know that the long poem or poem-sequence has always been an important presence. At readings too you always seem keen to make space for longer pieces. Could you say why you're attracted to the possibilities of the long poem?

MP: I think this goes back to the roots of my history as a writer...I started out to be a novelist and, in fact, it was while struggling with the novel, I first jotted down short poems as a relief from the long slog of a novel. The novel didn't (quite deservedly) get published - but the poems did. That's why, some years later, when I tried writing again I opted for poetry. But nearly all my poems are stories, and so, when I began to gain confidence, some had to get longer. It was only then that I began, of necessity, to explore techniques and recognise the imaginative potentials of the longer poem. It could be compared to switching from composing songs to writing concertos and then symphonies. Hope that doesn't sound too pretentious... The golden rule when working on any poem, and supremely important for a long one, is to constantly ask the question: *Is this boring*? I have the feeling that any poem has a natural length, whether three lines, three hundred - or three thousand. A poem tells me when to stop (more often that I shouldn't have even started). One of the great feelings I get, when I realise this is going to be a long one, is relief; for I'll be in for a lot of surprises, delight and disgust, but won't have to fret about trying to dig something up to write about for quite a while. They can be hard to get published but that makes for a bigger buzz when they are. It's an adventurous business; easy to throw away a short poem but sad when you realise you should bury a long one.

IP: The influence of Pablo Neruda has often been recognised in your work. Could you say something about why Neruda is such a significant - and abiding - presence? Who else would you say is important?

MP: The influence of Pablo Neruda is twofold: the poet and the man - and, of course, the two are really one. As a poet he has an exceptional ability to make the commonplace extraordinary, evocative; to make stones sing. This is why, when I'm stuck for inspiration, I can go to his poetry and, before I know what's happening, I'm into writing myself. His whole long life was devoted to poetry, and a crusade to ennoble the achievements of ordinary men and women and to relieve the injustices of their oppression. He risked his own life in the latter cause. Sometimes, his very passion may have overcome his poetic sensibility, but if that hadn't occurred he would have betrayed his honesty. Not a heinous fault, especially when this criticism may apply to only a small proportion of a huge volume of wondrous poetry. Enough, Shakespeare is a big influence - for the very poetry of his language and for his broad insights into humanity. In contrast to Neruda, his politics were disguised and, being a playwright, he concentrated more on the individual. These two great figures compliment each other admirably. Of present day poets, probably Ken Smith and Geoff Hattersley are the two I most admire. The other influences might be every poet I've ever read - for one reason or another. There are lessons to be learnt from what you judge to be success and equally from failure - one's own as well as others'.

IP: It's interesting that you mention Shakespeare in this context as he somehow manages to be expansive and intense at the same time... I'd like, for a moment, to concentrate on one poem - 'Rendezvous' from *In A Rare Time of Rain*. I'd want to know the sort of process that goes into something like that. How do you set about writing a poem?

MP: Ian, I wondered when a stinker like this would come. This is a poem that certainly can be said to be a 'mood' poem. I'm sure it came out of a rainy grey morning or in the early hours of a cold night. It's not - as it may appear - to come from an actual meeting but rather an imagined one. The other person in the poem is perhaps a composite of several people from my past... I can't remember how this poem came into being, the trigger for it. From a random thought or memory (surely it was written in autumn) it will have grown organically, scribbled on a scrap of paper from the tumblings in my brain. At some stage it will have begun to develop it's music and rhythms, which decided its form. Obviously, I got into nostalgic mode and was letting my mind zoom around the past because some of the imagery came from my memory bank. The purple stain on the glasses from a certain type of heavy

Spanish wine, the blue wind out of a clear Mediterranean sky when at sea, bones whitening in heather from walks on the Yorkshire moors or in the Highlands of Scotland, sharp as a shepherd's knife from when I worked on farms, are of specific memories coming out of the fog in my head. Other images were created in response to a need, raised by what was happening with the poem, rather than being something specifically recalled. This process is fascinating because the invented images then become concrete, while the remembered ones, because they are shifted from their actual context, become less so. This is only of relevance to the writer, not the reader. But how the whole thing came about, is and remains a mystery as far as I'm concerned. Just using the magic. Conventional logics serve their purpose in the final stages of ordering and refining a poem; if they drove it, it would be better in prose. On the other hand, you can say it's all logical. It's just a question of which and how many of the brain's processes are being used. An attempt to precisely define the makings of a poem is like trying to analyse a wind...

IP: I think it would be interesting at this point to ask you to say something about poetry readings. You seem perfectly happy, for instance, to read long poems - something many other poets won't risk. How do readings - which seem to me to be an important part of your approach to poetry - relate to your practice as a poet?

MP: Because I want my poems to work on both the written and oral levels, readings are important to me as they give me some indication of how successful they may be on at least one of these. This is particularly true of longer poems. I think it's easier to hold attention with a selection of shorter and varied pieces. If you notice attention flagging during a reading of a long one you're in trouble - there's something seriously amiss with either your presentation or the poem itself - or both! This is a valuable criticism. It's also a devastating and humbling experience to be halfway through your great masterpiece and the audience is snoring. Though I will certainly have read my poems to myself before, in performance I may still discover some things that need change. Hearing others read is also important in picking up tips to improve your own presentation and in noting pitfalls to be avoided. I always get irritated when a poet starts with an explanation of what a poem is 'about'.

Some relevant insights are ok but if I felt I had to explain a poem itself I'd be seriously concerned for it's health. I could get into the issue of 'on the page' and 'performance poetry' but I won't.
IP: It seems to me that 'City of Flowers' is the most representative of your poems - and it's good to see it published as just that, a long poem as a collection in itself. How do you manage the gear-changes that make a long poem interesting?

MP: I wouldn't like to think that I worked to a pre-determined formula. It's only when I've got going that I'll make decisions about form, framework... Mostly, I'll write it in small pieces as this helps to keep things tight. If I do get carried away with a longer bit of writing I'll leave the decision whether or not to serve it up whole or in parts until the pattern of the poem has emerged. But differing poems will induce differing techniques. If you compare 'City of Flowers' with 'The Man Who Had Forgotten The Names of Trees', in my latest collection *Caminate*, you'll notice a considerable difference in managing the gear-changes. In the first, the various themes are woven together, intertwined; while the latter goes with more of a run, with the ride made bumpy to break it up. Changing pace is important. I fear this give the impression of order and planning, whereas the real process is much more instinctive and only rationalised in hindsight. As mentioned in reply to an earlier question, a sort of musicality gets involved and much depends on the style, rhythms and instruments chosen. One day perhaps I'll produce something for a full orchestra - including cymbals, triangles, harps, organ grinder and monkey. Maybe I got nearest to that with 'City of Flowers'...

IP: Your most recent work demonstrates an increasing willingness to loosen the structures by ignoring established 'rules'. Do you find you have to invent new ones in order to give the poems some shape?

MP: I'm not aware of having invented anything, but rather adapted other ideas and methods that I've picked up consciously or subliminally. Whenever I get a different voice I feel that a form, structure and style, must be sought that is in keeping with that voice or those voices and their rhythms. I presume the recent work you refer to are some poems where I abandoned all punctuation, use of capitals, and employed unconventional and some phonetic spellings. This was to try to get over the feel of the scatterbrained musings and conversations that were the tone of these. Always a big decision for me with each poem or series of poems is what form will be used. What mood or voice am I in? And what suits that? The result is that I don't produce those neat volumes of poetry that seem so fashionable - all seriously consistent. My head's a nightmare of confusions; and so I'm always having to jump from one set of 'rules' to another. I wouldn't be honest if I wrote otherwise. Perhaps this is why I'm partial to longer poems - I get some order into chaos. I've tremendous respect for all that's gone before in poetry and what's happening today. But when it comes down to the clinched wire, the only 'rule' is what works - what can I get away with, and that's for others to judge. There must be the courage to have a go but I doubt if fortune always favours the brave. I hope I can continue having a good laugh at myself when I fall on my arse.

IP: How important is autobiography to an inventive imagination like yours?

MP: Of course, all that has happened in life will effect one way or another, what is written. I rarely, if ever, write autobiographically in the sense of describing particular events from my past but, like a novelist, will draw on recollections of people and places and events; but not necessarily used in their original settings, and the people are - more often than not - composites. Sometimes a glimpse from memory may give me the idea for a poem that will take off from there. For instance, the poem called 'Top Hold' came from a strong memory of a particular moment when, standing in a high pass in the Andes, I looked out over the great ocean of green of the Amazonian rain forest. Recalling this years later, I then pictured a man in such a spot and imagined what he saw in his mind's eye as he faced each direction. The result was a mixture of the real and the imagined. You may notice that I switched from the first person to the third. This, I feel, gives me more freedom - releases me even further from the restrictions of memory. I hold it to be essential not to get trapped into the reality of recollection or, indeed, of the present. As in painting, the artist must have the freedom to ignore, to a lesser or greater extent, the particularities of reality in order to explore it. This is beginning to sound like a lot of guff... What I mean is I like flying. Writing poetry is an adventure and merely recording the past is hardly that.

IP: We've talked up now about poetry as an isolated art form. I know you've worked closely with jazz musicians in the past. Could you say, in conclusion, what attracts you to jazz and why you feel it works so well alongside poetry in performance?

MP: From some of my previous answers you'll have noticed how important I feel the affinity between poetry and music to be. It may be I'm a frustrated musician... Why jazz/blues works so well because improvisation is so basic to the music. Musicians can work from the 'feel' of the poem and to a greater extent, the poet can respond to the music. Little or no rehearsal is required. Your question mentioned working alongside poetry. I would expect it to be much more integrated than that. One other plus about performing with musicians is that you'll get a different audience. Most poetry readings appear to be almost entirely inhabited by people who write poems (or review them). It's both refreshing and challenging to have your stuff presented to 'normal' people - it can be both exhilarating and humbling.

IP: Thanks for that, Milner. I owe you a pint.

André Mangeot *NATURAL CAUSES.*
Shoestring Press. 36pp. £6.50.
ISBN 1-899549 86 2

André Mangeot enjoys a career in performance as a member of The Joy of Six, a poetry troupe now producing serious work on the page. As far as I know *Natural Causes* is his first slim collection, produced by the admirable Shoestring Press of John Lucas. Lucas knows humane talent when he sees it and Mangeot is a serious find. His subjects are mostly the result of observation, watching life's movements without any particular privileging of his personal experience. So there are poems about cars being vandalised, about men working on the road, about the training run of a small-time boxer, all presented with a sharp eye, a good sense of narrative shape, and, best of all, a kind of common, affectionate music, as in 'Billy Poole' the boxer, with his:

> vaseline or spit
> of words to get him through another round,
> another day of digging ditches, mucking out
> or lugging bales in flat-iron heat for hirers
> locked to a medieval wage, backing fenmen
> into corners, onto ropes - and them still taking it.

There is something here of the early Douglas Dunn, a faint touch of Causley and a hint of Armitage in the form and wryness - that at least, is the general area - but the way the voice yields to the subject is Mangeot's own.

He is also good at unwinding an apparently minor but emblematic verse-sized story. 'Blood & Sand,' an anecdote about a colleague's love affair, is handled in rhymed quatrains, but lightly and playfully, so that the tough, sad, desolation of the event is warmed in the handling. His detail can be sensuous without being cloying as in 'Excitement Can Kill You,' *describing the green glide of silk and how the wells of your collarbone / led to your breasts - / and from there / to the rest of our lives.* That could be awkward or mawkish, but it is neither.

Other autobiographical poems include a sequence about taking a son with Asperger's Syndrome on holiday, a fine sestina about communication with his father, and intense moments of domestic life. Mangeot, to his credit, rarely falls into the trap of writing material that will simply create a good impression. The worst that could be said of his more overtly ‘feel-good’ work, such as the last poem in the book, is that it takes its own joy a little too much for granted. The short eight line poem, arranged into four couplets, sets up a figure in the frost, who opens his arms, and roars at the stars. It ends,

> The echo receded, revived -
> came back like a kiss
> from the galaxies, a kiss
> that said, Yes, you’re alive.

There is no doubting its honesty of feeling. I just wonder whether that is enough. One must struggle sometimes not to be loved. Poetry demands it. But this is a small cavil. *Natural Causes* is a very impressive collection and Mangeot a welcome voice of which, I feel pretty sure, we shall hear much more.

Reviewed by George Szirtes

BLAST: 48pp £4.50 ISBN 0-907123-39-2 (2002)
LET YOUR LEFT HAND SING: 38pp £3.99 ISBN 0-907123-79-1 (2003)
RACER: 32pp £3.99 ISBN 0-907123-44-9 (2003)
All published by Five Leaves Publications

These Five Leaves Publications are attractive, pocket-book editions of Kevin Fegan’s self-styled dramatic poems, giving the reader the opportunity to enjoy what was originally written for performance or radio. Fegan is a strong writer and it is good to see here subjects not immediately associated as being poetic, tackled so proficiently.

Blast was first broadcast by BBC Radio Drama on 18th June 2001 and first performed at Contact Theatre in association with Manchester Poetry Festival on 12th November 2002. In *Blast* Fegan explores the poetry to be found in heavy industry and has chosen as his subject one of the heaviest – steel. Taking as his starting point the four elements: *I am consumed by fire,/ I am drowning in water,/ I am buried in earth,/ I am falling through the air* this is the story of a retired steelworker from a melting shop in South Yorkshire, *the fourteen furnaces of Templeborough,/ a cathedral of a place,/the biggest melting shop in the world* from a time when it was a *Job for life, wife for life,/that's the way it's supposed to be.*

Fegan skilfully interweaves the details of the man's family life with that of the foundry and of the four elements. *Where there are mills you'll always find water,... We did most of our courting by the river... Once we fell in ...Her clothes were so wet I could see /the outline of her body ... Water assumes the shape of the vessel/in which it is contained.* And most poignantly ... *the day our son died./Inside we lined up in pews/in front of a furnace,/aware how dangerously close we are/ to our own mortality.*

But in the end there are *No regrets, if I could/do it all over again, I would.... I am purged by the fire,/I am floating on the water,/ I am embraced by the earth, /I am flying through the air.*

Fegan has taken a difficult environment to experiment with in writing, but has produced a memorable performance piece. The narrative is complemented by colour and black and white photographs, which were taken from an anonymous set of slides found in a skip outside the closed down Templeborough melting shop.

In *Let Your Left Hand Sing* elements of autobiography are fused with five stories of displacement and migration, bringing the 'global village' to 'East Midlands Street'. Taking the concept of differences - *I was born left-handed:/these things happen and ... We don't choose where in the world/we are born.* Fegan gives us histories of six people's lives up to the present day.
Kevin introduces himself at the beginning, with details of his birth and parentage, and his narrative is interwoven throughout the book. Being left-handed *I was writing with the wrong hand... They forced me to turn my back/ on my own culture,/to be like them, ...but what really matters/is what I have to say/which comes from within/and finds its own way.* With this concept in mind we are given stories from different cultural backgrounds about people who have eventually come to live in the East Midlands. The most satisfying, I found, was Nirmalas' Story which tells the journey of a Hindu woman from Delhi, whose life takes her to Poona, then to Malawi where she marries and loses *all my childhood freedom*, then on to England and Leicester *...a tolerant/multi-cultural society* and who says of the River Soar, down by Castle Gardens ... *it's time we consecrated/this short*

stretch of the river, ... somehow we're meant to be here. Zanta is an Acholi from the Sudan. Hers is a harrowing story. From her home in Derby she says *I was eight years old when the soldiers came,/...don't ask me what happened to my father,/don't ask me what they did to my left hand ...* Tarasz's Story is one of a Ukraine who *came here after the War* and whose bitterness is felt in every line. *no one ever tames Cossack. ... there is only one/land of the free – Ukraine. ... but I cannot ever go back there again.*

What I like about this book, which resulted from a commission for the *Long Journey Home* festival, is the apparent honesty of Fegan's own story and the wonderful snippets of information he gives, for example: *there are eighty-seven distinct terms of abuse/for left-handers in this country alone ... a ligature was tied around/the left testicle to restrict/the birth of a female child in favour of/a male child ...* My only reservation is that these stories have an individuality whose different voices would be enhanced in performance, but on the page can read with too much similarity.

But in the words of Paul, a prisoner who has ... *lived in seventeen different towns/yet I have seen none of them.* the strength of this book is that *I've met some wonderful people along the way.*

Racer is an exciting story of the Isle of Man TT. Written as a fast-paced narrative, Fegan her defines his interpretation of the dramatic poem: a prose poem *A simple twist of the wrist/results in a surge of adrenaline/as I pull away from the start line/into a 100 m.p.h. wheelie ...* containing elements of pure poetry *Know me as the Crow,/not the common carrion kind/but a hooded Crow of Celtic origin...* with an occasional smattering of full and half-rhyme. Commissioned by BBC Radio 4 Drama *Racer* was first broadcast on 9th December 2002. We are taken, bend-by-bend, on as thrilling a ride round this most famous of motorcycle road-race circuits as words can capture and convey. *Concentrate, that's the key./When I race the TT, I feel/an overwhelming sense of cheating death,/it's like robbing a locksmiths,/the risk and the pleasure/of an immoral victory.* During the race we learn of the life and loves of The Racer as he makes this final attempt at the championship he has always craved. Written with clarity and simplicity this is a 200 mph read where you are with him to the end *I will not live in the past,/I will not live forever,/I am alive, this is what matters.*

Reviewed by Jeremy Duffield

Seven League Stilettos
Jane Kinninmont
Ragged Raven Press
ISBN 0 9542397 6 8 £7

This is a book that opens its arms and welcomes you in. From the first to the last, this is a collection of highly accessible poems. That is not to say they lack depth, Kinninmont explores the big themes – life, love, loss and survival – beloved of poets since time immemorial, but she does this in a very readable way.

Many of the poems feel anchored in the personal and this makes them real and honest in their content. Her treatment of suicide for example; shows an understanding of the need for dark humour in the "public perception" 'Dismal thoughts from Archway Road' and the need for compassion in the harsh reality and aftermath of "successful" and "unsuccessful" experience. For Lee and Children's Ward

My particular favourite is 'Children's Ward', which explores something of the confusion such acts create:

> We were the same age. We didn't know what to do
> and we had brought too many words, too many
> presents and sweets, and the nurses disliked us, our laughter,
> which we only meant as medicine.
> So many of us try to die, they lose patience.

Many of the pieces are love poems. They speak in a clear romantic voice of the companionship and joy of being in love – of the sharing that takes place between lovers. I found myself thinking, "I wish I had written that", and that's always a good sign on my personal like/dislike barometer.

> the world lets go of you too -
> the normal rules and laws loosen their grip –
>
> and I can cross any distance in no time at all
> striding continents in love's seven league stilettos.

It's not all good of course, for me it lacked any feminist bite, and a couple of the poems felt like they didn't work on the page (though may well do so in performance), but still an impressive first collect and one I shall encourage my friends to go out and buy.

Review by Sue Allen

The New Girls
Sue Dymoke
Shoestring Press
ISBN 1 904886 00 0 £7.95

This is a beautiful, intelligent and thought provoking collect of poetry, in which, each piece has something of it's own to say.
When I reached the end, I felt like I had been enjoying a conversation with a friend, and was sorry that it was now over. It is a self-assured work, with a confidence born of knowing one's craft. The voice within it is clear and lyrical.

There is a strong sense of belonging here, a sense of reminiscence and memory, which at times is clearly personal, but which holds within it shared cultural memory that many could relate to. As I read this book, I was put in mind of American Memory Quilts, in which the important moments in the life of the family are sewn together and kept as treasures; swatches of material from wedding gowns and christening robes combined into personal landscapes of experience. Dymoke does this with words, building a patchwork of language which is a joy to behold, and has enduring appeal. It is a book I know I shall return to many times in the future.

Review by Sue Allen

The Weight of Cows
Mandy Coe
Shoestring Press
ISBN 1-899549-97-8 £7.95

There is something kaleidoscopic about Mandy Coe's poetry. It is as if she can tackle almost any subject and make it sparkle. This is not to say there is anything glitzy or superficial about her work. Even at her most earnest – exercising her historical imagination, exploring a mythos or willing us to empathies with the generally unsung – there is always an imaginative freshness of vision in play. Take, for example, 'Settlers' which begins:

> As if this land was a fractious baby,
> people came to settle it. Wet-nurses
> reeking of fog and coal, they emptied carpet-bags
> of cotton and gin, unrolled a sing-song tongue
> that twisted the names of gods and mountains.

Startling image to begin with, then the swift move into sensuous detail, then the gripping 'unrolled a sing-song tongue/that twisted'. If that doesn't make you read on, nothing will, you're a lost cause. Or this from 'Souls':

> Dying is best done out doors
> if souls are to rise without entanglement
> in lampshades and louvre blinds.

This should make you want immediately to go out and buy the book!

And if her poems open well they also pursue sure trajectories to satisfying endings. At a time when there are so many poems around which just seem – portentously – to stop in mid-air, Mandy Coe's poems emotionally, thoughtfully, satisfyingly get there, they say what they have to say. 'Settlers' ends with:

> The first home was abandoned,
> then another. Straight lines
> blurred under weeds and animal tracks.
> Barn doors swung open, banging
> like the heels of a sulky child.

And sometimes they startle, touching a nerve or a tickle spot, by shifting perspective. For instance, in 'Her Domain', a poem which, behind the scenes, asks questions about the relationship between art and life, we find a woman at the mirror making up her face, polishing her nails:

> Leaning back, she angles
> her head from side to side.
> It is done. As she twists the lipstick
> from its black and gold case,
> the child at her shoulder
> makes a silent 'O' with her mouth.

Yet again, in 'Cathedral Tower, a poem which perfectly re-enacts the sensations of climbing up and then back down a spiral stone-staircase, we end with:

> On a bench a sandwich
> is being unwrapped. You bite into it,
> squinting at the sky, already
> doubting you were ever up there.

Absolutely!

Rest assured I haven't just picked out best bits as examples: simply chosen them at random. If you find them persuasive, rewarding, consider them as typical. There are no dud poems, verses, lines in this collection.

The poems do what good poems should: they refresh our vision of the world and the things we, for the most part, take for granted; they make us see the ordinary as extraordinary; oblige us to look again with our (abandoned or forgotten) childlike perception. The child *under the table/where I hid among the smell of knees, worrying*, the window-cleaner's 'shammies,/pale as scrambled egg, soft as something sinful', the shoe-shop girls coveting stiletto-heels *so high and sharp, that wherever/you walked you left a perforated line*, or in a marvellous poem about staring *Train windows are useful for bending stares/round corners.* But only heavenly misted glass/prevents them from being sensed' (consider the fineness of that enjambement *bending stares/round corners!*). These make us see, undergo a realisation, experience a truth.

And the poems also have an attractive, quirky sense of humour. In Off Course a girl blows her boyfriend a goodbye kiss which *never arrived./With a gust of wind off the Mersey/it went off course* : the poem ends:

> Only been gone five minutes
> and she's kissing other men already.

'Staring for Beginners' ends on a caution:

> Tip: gazing and staring are two different things.
> It is vital to remember this in relationships, especially
> when your partner is naked.

Kaleidoscopic then. Clear-eyed, thoughtful, amusing. But, above all, poems that really work. Real poems.

Review by Matt Simpson

Biographies

Tony Flynn, (b. 1951) studied Philosophical Theory at Hull University. His poems first appeared in *A Rumoured City: New Poets from Hull* and in *A Strange Routine*. Since then further collections have been published by Bloodaxe.

Peter Dale became a freelance writer in 1993. His selected poems, *Edge to Edge*, was published by Anvil (1997) He has translated Latorgue, Villon and Dante. After editing *Agenda* his is now poetry editor for *Oxford Today*. His latest collection, *Under the Breath* has been published by Anvil.

Jessica Philips (b. 1985, Luton) now lives in Liverpool and is studying English, Ancient History and Archaeology at The University of Liverpool.

Alan Dunnett (b.1953) read English at Oxford before going to drama school. After some years as a freelance theatre director, he moved into training; recently being made Course Director, MA Performance, at Drama Centre London. His poems have appeared in *Orbis, The Interpreter's House, Stand,* and *The Rialto* among others.

Paul Nicholson lives and writes in York.

Ece Sakar (b. 1959, Izmir, Turkey) After getting her B.Sc. degree in Educational Science at the Middle East Technical University she has worked as Copywriter, columnist, interviewer, editor and counselor for various advertisement companies and the Turkish National TV Channel TRT. Though all of her writings are in Turkish, she can only write poems in English. Sakar currently is working on a bilingual (Turkish – English) book on the *Theory of Knowledge.*

Louise Mansfield lives and wries in Yorkshire; this is the first time a poem of hers has appeared in a literary magazine.

Amari Hamadene (b. 1968, Chief, Algeria) directs currently the Press & Communication Agency Arabesque which he founded in 1999, and the literary magazine, *Arabesques.* His poetry has been widely published in France, Luxemburg and Belgium. This is the first time it's appeared in an UK journal.

Helen Goodway started writing mostly poetry four years ago. Also has written plays, one of which was performed at the Pleasants in Edinburgh (2001). Currently she is the principal English editor of *Tadeeb* – a platform and conduict of both Urdu and English, and is working on a biogaphy of Faiz Ahmed Faiz,

David Constantine (Oxford, UK) is a well-published & celebrated poet, critic & translator. A Fellow of Queen's College, Oxford, he recently has translated Goethe's *Faust* (Penguin Classic). His Selected Poems appeared in 1991; his latest collection is *Something for the Ghosts* (Bloodaxe 20020. For the last two years a poem of his has been short-listed for the Forward Prize for Poetry in the single poem category. David Constantine is interviewed in this issue of *Dream Catcher.*

Anne Brechin is currently taking a sabbatical before completing her final year at Durham University, studying philosophy and psychology.

Claire Sharpe began an MA in Creative Writing at the University of East Anglia in September 2004. Her poems have appeared in *Pulsar, South* and *Staple.*

Antony Nicholls' work has appeared in *Ambit, Acumen, Staple, the Interpreter's House, Tumbscrew* and *The Shop.*

Philip Burton, in recent years, has had many poems published in literary arts magazines, including in: *PN Review, Other Poetry, Orbis, The Frogmore Papers, Prism International* (Canada), *Poetry Nottingham International* and *Swansea Review.* His pamphlet collections – *Quarrelling Along the Camber, The Raven's Diary, Places Off the Map* and *Blue Grass* – have been praised by poets such as Don Paterson and Catherine Smith.

Alessio Zanelli (b. 1963) lives in Cremona, Lombardy where he works as a private financial advisor. He has writtein in English since 1985His most recent collection is *Small Press Verses & Poeticonjectures* (Xlibris, 2002). He is a member of the Poetry Society of London.

Jeremy Gadd is Australian and has contributed articles, 50 short stories and 150 poems to literary magazines and periodicals in Australia, the UK, the USA, India and Germany. UK magazines include: *Poetry Wales, Staple, Poetry and Audience, Tears in the Fence* and *Iota*. He has also had his plays professionally produced in Australia.

Lucy Brennan: (b. Dublin) immigrated to Canada (1957). Her poetry has been well-received by Canadian UK and Irish journals. Her full collection *Migrants All* is published by WaterShed (1999, Toronto, Canada)

Miles Salter: writes and lives in York, England.

Gloria Moreno-Castillo spent most of her life in Spain. Now retired she lives in South London. She's had poems published in *The Express, The Interpreter's House, Weyfarers, Reach, Links, Iota, Other Poetry, Poetry Cornwall* and *Poetry Nottingham International,* as well as *BuzzWords*, *The Reader and Connections,* She reviews poetry for *Reach* and *Orbis*.

Julia Davis is a frequent contributor to *Dream Catcher.* As well he poems have appeared in *Poetry Greece, Brando's Hat, Pennine Platform* and *Stovepipe* (USA). She collaborates with international composers and theatre directors to create performance pieces of poetry, drama and music.

Brian Biddle is a member of the Toddington Poetry Society. His poems have appeared in *The Interpreter's House* and twice in *Ambit* and a range of other magazines.

André Mangeot's short stories and poems have appeared in UK and American publications (incl. *London Magazine, TLS, Daily Express, The Dark Horse, Chiron Review, Pearl* and *Rattapallax*). His collection *Natural Causes* (Shoestring Press, 2003) is reviewed in this issue of *Dream Catcher.* A new collection *Mixer* is due in early 2005. He is a member of the performance group Joy of Six (www.joyofsix.co.uk)

Philip Foster works as a Basic Skill Coordinator for a Housing Association. He's a founder member of the Albert Poets (Huddersfield) running workshops, organizing readings and putting together anthologies.

Rani Drew (Cambridge) writes short stories and poems that have been published in various UK and North American poetry and fiction magazines. A playwright she has written plays and radio plays producing them in the UK, China and Hungary.

Joolz Denby (Bradford), a frequent contributor to *Dream Catcher,* has four collections; her latest *Errors of the Spirit* (Flambard). Her first novel *Stone Baby* won the New Crime Writer of the Year Award and her second *Corazon* has been highly praised. She is a constant performer with a worldwide following her tours have taken her recently to South Africa, Canada and Germany.

Gregory Gilbert Grumbs was born on the Dutch Caribbean Island of Aruba and grew up on St. Martin/St Maarten. In the Netherlands, where he studied and worked, many of his poems have appeared anthologies and magazines. He's been published in the UK (e.g. *The Interpreter's House, Pennine Platform*), in France, the Caribbean and Japan. In the USA, where he now lives, his work has appeared in an important college anthology and in magazines such as *The Ear* and *Rockhurst Review*.

Kathryn Daszkiewicz was born and brought up in the north east but now lives and works in Lincolnshire. She has had poems in various magazines including *The Rialto, The Frogmore Papers* and *Mslexia. Kathryn* was awarded a bursary by East Midlands Arts in 2001 and a selection of her work appeared in the 2001 *Shoestring Press* New Writing published that year. She recently took part in the 24 – 8 tour of East Midlands writers and has read her work at various venues around the region and beyond.
Owen Gallagher is a primary teacher. His collection *Sat Guru Snowman* was published by Peterloo Poets. He received a major award from The London Arts Board towards his second collection.

Idris Caffrey (b. Rhayader, Wales) lives in Tamworth. A fifth poetry collection, *Departures and Returns* (Peer Poetry International, 2002) is available from 26 Arlinton House, Bath Street, Bath BA1 1QN.

Robin Lindsay Wilson - a playwright and theatre director living in Glasgow – has had poems in *The Riatlo, Iota, Links, Orbis* and *Magma*. A selection of his work has recently appeared in *Dream State* (Polygon), anthology of new Scottish writers.

Ruth Anna Latta (Ottawa, Canada) won a Canadian Author's Association competition (2003); 'Keeping Faith' appeared in *Quality Fiction for Women*, (Rugby, UK). With five other books, her collection of short stories, *Save the Last dance for Me*, is published by Poetica Press, Ottawa, 2002.

Kate Potts lives in South East London and works in music publishing. She has an MA in creative and life writing from Goldsmith College, London.

Stephen Parr (b. 1946, Darwen, Lancashire) moved to London (1966) to join the BBC as a sound engineer. Writing poetry since the 1970s, he's appeared in many small press magazines, with ten self-published pamphlets of poetry; his poems were in Bloodaxe's landmark anthology *The Long Pale Corridor.* He published his first full collection *North of the Future* in 1999.

Adrian Buckner is a poet, reviewer and adult education tutor whose work has appeared in various magazines such as *London Magazine, Frogmore Papers and Acumen.* He is a revew editor for *Staple*.

Gordon Wilson teaches English and Creative Writing at Franklin College, Grimsby. His poems have appeared in *Staple, Poetry Nottingham International* and *Envoi* as well as *Dream Catcher* issue 12.

Amyon Corbould, a Londoner living in Grimsby, has been published in 'bluechrome anthology' and won the last year's Lincolnshire's Humour in Poetry Competition judged by Wendy Cope. She runs the Stitchworts poetry group and belongs to Grimsby Writers.

Mike Barlow's first full collection *Living On The Difference* was overall winner of the Poetry Business Book and Pamphlet Competition 2003: to be published in October 2004 by Smiths Doorstop.

David Gill (b. 1934) studied German and French at University College London. He has written poetry continuously since 15 and in the 1960s was published by Chatto and Windus: *Men Without Evenings & The Pagada and Other Poems.* Along with his work appearing in many magazines he has translated the Lachian poet Ondra Lysohorsky. Recently he's published small print-runs of his own verse: *A Little Colleteral Damage* (Iraq war) and *The Cemetery of Pleasures* (written in Portugal).

Hubert Moore: is a well-established poet. His collection *Touching Down in Utopia* (Shoestring Press, 2002) was reviewed in *Dream Catcher issue 11.* His pamphlet Beautifully Kept things was a joint winner of the Poetry Business Competition (2003).

Mario Susko is a witness and survivor of the war in Bosnia, having left Sarajevo in March 1993. After eight months at UEA he moved to the US, where he had lived, on and off, half of the last 32 years. During the war he escaped three mortar attacks, finding he was less than twenty meters away. He was wounded and pulled out from under a wall when a third projectile, a 155 mm. shell, had exploded in his room. Living in a cellar for two and a half months in Dobrinja settlement, he witnessed the cleansing of Dobrinja's Section IV in May 1992. By phone, his only connection to the outside world, he gave numerous interviews to journalists, from Herald Tribune to UPI, reporting about the dealings of the UNPROFOR officials and Serbs in Lukavica garrison. He conducted surrealistic communication with the first UNPROFOR commander in Sarajevo, also taping an eight-minute message to the US Congress via the American Embassy in Belgrade in June. Pulled out of the settlement in August to the center of the city, he later foraged for food and water, twice shot at by snipers, before leaving the city. His private library of over 5000 books was looted and burned, many of his books later were sold on the streets of Sarajevo.

Of a somewhat mysterious origin, Mario Susko, a grandson of a Ukrainian wanderer and an Italian from a line of sea explorers, was born in Sarajevo, only to spend his first ten years among the dirt and dust, coal and steel of the industrial town of Zenica. Experiencing hunger after WWII and illness, including para-typhus, he moved to Sarajevo to live with his aunt, a famous stage actress, when his father, after the years of horrific abuse, left his mother.

He graduated in English from the University of Sarajevo followed by graduate studies in comparative literature in Zagreb; then entered a graduate programme at SUNY at Stony Brook and received his M.A. and Ph.D. in the 1970s.

He is a three time Fulbright scholar, a GVSU visiting scholar, twice a stipendist of the British Council, as well as a visiting fellow at the University of East Anglia, Norwich.

He has published 66 books: 22 books of his poems. He has edited and translated several anthologies, including a an anthology of contemporary British poetry (1988, ed. together with David Harsent), contemporary American poetry (1990), 20th century American short stories (1986 & 1990); also, fiction by Donald Barthelme (1985), and poems by Theodore Roethke (1982) and e. e. cummings (1988). Other books include a volume of essays on John Donne, W. B. Yeats, Wallace Stevens, among others *The Spirit and the Clay* (1978) and many translations of American and some British writers, including: Saul Bellow, E. L. Doctorow, William Styron, J. G. Ballard and Kurt Vonnegut.

Since 1994, his poems have been published in 43 U.S. magazines: *Borderlands, Poetry International, Seneca Review, Fence, Verse, Glass Tesseract, The Progressive, Chase Park* and *Phantasmagoria.*

He is the recipient of several awards; recently the 1993/94 Council of Europe Award for Literary Translators, the 1997 Nassau Review Poetry Award, the 1998 Premio Internazionale di Poesia e Letteratura Nuove Lettere (Naples, Italy), the 2000 Tin Ujevic Award (Zagreb,Croatia) for *Versus Exsul* - best book of poems published in Croatia 1999 and the 2003 Chancellor's Award (SUNY, State of New York) for Excellence in Scholarship and Creative Activities, with three books of poems published in the US: *Mothers, Shoes and Other Mortal Songs* (1995), *Versus Exsul* (1998), and *The Life After* (2001). His new book will be released by Turtle Point Press in 2005. Most recent books include a Croatian edition of *The Life After* (Zagreb: Meandar, 2002), his integral edition/translation of Walt Whitman's *Leaves of Grass* (Zagreb: Meandar, 2002), and selected poems 1982-2002, *Reading Life and Death* (Zagreb: Meandar, 2003).